Chinese TV in the Netflix Era

Chinese TV in the Netflix Era

Edited by
Xiaying Xu (Richard Xu) and Hui Liu

ANTHEM PRESS

Anthem Press
An imprint of Wimbledon Publishing Company
www.anthempress.com

This edition first published in UK and USA 2023
by ANTHEM PRESS
75–76 Blackfriars Road, London SE1 8HA, UK
or PO Box 9779, London SW19 7ZG, UK
and
244 Madison Ave #116, New York, NY 10016, USA

© 2023 Xiaying Xu (Richard Xu), Hui Liu
editorial matter and selection;
individual chapters © individual contributors

The moral right of the authors has been asserted.

All rights reserved. Without limiting the rights under copyright reserved above, no part of this publication may be reproduced, stored or introduced into a retrieval system, or transmitted, in any form or by any means (electronic, mechanical, photocopying, recording or otherwise), without the prior written permission of both the copyright owner and the above publisher of this book.

British Library Cataloguing-in-Publication Data
A catalogue record for this book is available from the British Library.

Library of Congress Control Number: 2022922288
A catalog record for this book has been requested.

ISBN-13: 978-1-83998-705-2 (Hbk)
ISBN-10: 1-83998-705-7 (Hbk)

Cover Credit: Yancheng Zhang

This title is also available as an e-book.

CONTENTS

Introduction   vi
Xiaying Xu

Chapter 1.   Webisode Distribution and Globalization Strategies of Video-Streaming Platforms: Taking iQIYI as an Example   1
Zhixia Mo and Hui Liu

Chapter 2.   The Production of High-Quality Homemade Short Dramas on Chinese Networks: The Example of iQIYI's Mist Theater   19
Jia Xian and Qinqin Ren

Chapter 3.   What Are They Bullet-Screening About? A Content Analysis of Bullet Screen Comments about *Crime Crackdown* (2021)   37
Xiaying Xu and Qingyuan Zhao

Chapter 4.   Content, Platforms and Distribution: Challenges and Prospect in the Field of Webisode Productions   57
Wei Jiang and Pengcheng Zhou

Notes on Contributors   83

Index   85

INTRODUCTION

Xiaying Xu

Is Netflix officially available in China? No, it is not. However, there are 253,484 ratings for the first season of *Sex Education* (2019) on Douban, one of China's biggest community websites. Equally familiar to Chinese audiences are *House of Cards* (2013) and *Emily in Paris* (2020), as well as HBO series *Westworld* (2016–2022), or the Disney series *Black Widow* (2021).

Subscription-video-on-demand (SVOD) services are available on many online video-streaming platforms (VSPs) in China, such as iQIYI, Youku and Tencent Video, backed by Baidu, Alibaba and Tencent (BAT) groups, respectively. The video content on these platforms can be the same shows as those broadcasted on national or provincial television stations, or originally produced and exclusively streamed on the VSP. Meanwhile, VSPs purchase the distribution rights of foreign films and television series to enrich the content pool. By way of example, the first season of the U.S. sitcom *Friends* (1994) is now available on Tencent Video. The content on VSPs can be viewed on a computer screen, iPad, or cell phone or be streamed via a TV box on the back of the television screen, facilitated by 4G or 5G networks. Many audiences may not sit in front of the TV screen with family members and may prefer watching content alone on a screen of their own and interacting with other viewers through bullet screen comments. As Michael Curtin has suggested, television is "no longer a broadcast medium or a network medium, or even a multichannel medium; television had become a matrix medium, an increasingly flexible and dynamic mode of communication," characterized by "interactive exchanges, multiple sites of productivity and diverse modes of interpretation and use" (Curtin 2009, 13).

This book aims to provide an account of Chinese television, particularly online drama series, or webisodes, with an awareness of the existence and competition of Netflix. Currently, Chinese VSPs of webisodes cannot defeat Netflix in terms of production value, nor can they be like Netflix, as is the case for its Belgian alternative (Raats & Evans 2021). We can analyze the strategies that these VSPs deployed for survival and development. As of December 2012, the number of internet users in China reached one billion, among which 99.7 percent go online through mobile phones, and 33 percent through televisions (CNNIC 2021, 11–17). However, as Zhao Jing (2017) has argued, the media convergence of broadcasting, telecommunications and the Internet is far more complicated than technology convergence. It involves negotiations of power relations, commercial interests and national cultural security concerns. What is available to the one billion internet users watching webisodes today is achieved through "bumpy roads towards convergence."

Traditional models of TV drama distribution are being transgressed. China Central Television (CCTV) and provincial stations no longer dominate the market. TV drama release schedules have changed from "TV station first, internet later" strategies to synchronous schedules, or even "internet first, TV station later" strategies (Fan & Chen 2021, 8). Audiences aged from 18 to 30 represent 67.2 percent of the audience of TV dramas online (ibid, 5). The relationship between state administration and VSP marketization is by no means straightforward or easy to grasp. It is a consensus among Chinese television scholars that there is a paradox between implementing a neoliberal strategy of marketization and maintaining control over ideology and national cultural security (Zhao 1998; Fung 2009; Wang & Lobato 2009). TV drama production and consumption are at the center of this paradoxical relationship.

Producing original drama series is one of the most effective ways for a VSP to make a difference in the competition for subscribers. However, what constitutes original production is complicated. In an in-depth study of Netflix's original content, Hidalgo et al. (2021) draw four categories of original content of Netflix: original production, continuations, co-productions, and acquired rights. Original production refers to "content originally produced by the company, usually through a strategic alliance with private producers," such as *Stranger Things* (2016). Continuations refer to "the company, within its own production catalog, picks up again shows that were originally broadcast on another television channel and creates new seasons, in search of the expansion of a previously tested success." Co-production means Netflix allies itself with television channels from different countries that become partners when producing content, aiming at supporting the local product that will later be distributed globally. Acquired rights refer to shows that "have been broadcast in different territories and exclusive distribution rights have been bought to broadcast them in other countries" Hidalgo et al. (2021, 2). As the authors point out, the commitment to producing original content is a key characteristic of Netflix. Something similar is going on with the Chinese VSPs. Though a majority of the content on Chinese VSPs is purchased or imported: there are a lot more quality content that can be imported than domestically produced, the production of original content is becoming a central battlefield for Chinese VSPs to establish their market status. The three major VSPs in China: iQIYI of Baidu, Tencent Video of Tencent and Youku of Alibaba, have all invested a lot in original content production with their own focuses. For example, iQIYI's Mist Theater series responded to the heavily criticized phenomenon of lengthy and redundant drama series that are broadcast on television channels with their original production of the Mist Theater series which are about twelve episodes on average with compact plots and high production values. Tencent Video's original drama production is more "popular" because they feature more idols and celebrity actors and actresses.

In the Chinese context, original content may also appear in many formats: original productions, adaptations, co-productions, acquired, which are similar to Netflix. In addition, VSPs also fight for exclusive broadcast rights. For example, Youku exclusively broadcasts *Day and Night* (2017), a suspense drama produced by a couple of other companies. It was so successful that Netflix later acquired it and distributed it on Netflix's own platform globally.

Day and Night (2017) thus offers a perfect example of "webisodes." It takes the Internet as the main communication medium. But the concept of "webisode" is also not clear-cut. It's an evolving concept. According to Merriam-Webster Dictionary, a webisode is "an episode especially of a TV show that may or may not have been telecast but can be viewed at a website" (Merriam-Webster.com 2022). The case is, it does not have to be a TV show. According to Wikipedia, a webisode is "an episode of a series that is distributed as part of a web series or on streaming television." (Wikipedia 2022) This definition has no mention of co-productions and co-distribution cases: some series are streamed online and broadcast on a TV channel simultaneously in China, sometimes with variations in content as deemed fit for the media, such as *The Thunder* (2019). For this book, the Wikipedia definition will work unless specially clarified.

The four chapters of this book focus on various issues regarding television studies in China. In Chapter 1, Hui Liu and Zhixia Mo focus on the iQIYI platform. As Wilfred Yang Wang and Ramon Lobato (2009) argue, a key difference between iQIYI and Netflix is that the critical concepts of a Western VSP, such as individualization, decentralization, user empowerment and disruption, cannot be readily applied to the Chinese context. This does not mean that the algorithm is not used in the content recommendation system. Chinese VSPs will recommend content to their users based on their watching history, but that is not the only interface formation mechanism. Liu and Mo offer a genealogy of the development of VSPs in China and a detailed and nuanced description of the business model and logic of iQIYI. Another contribution of this chapter is the discussion of the affordances of the iQIYI platform in providing services other than an intelligent video portal, and how that serves to sustain the development and positioning of iQIYI. Finally, given that Netflix is an international player, this chapter identifies possible target audiences of iQIYI productions in the global market, with reasonable precautions.

In Chapter 2, Jia Xian and Qinqin Ren focus on the core arena of competition among VSPs in China: original productions exclusively streamed on their own platform or jointly broadcasted on satellite TV stations. As subscription becomes a major source of income for VSPs, an effective strategy for attracting subscribers is that of showing one or two episodes of a television series to viewers for free and leaving it to the viewer to decide whether they would like to pay the subscription fee to continue watching the show or fight their own curiosity over what happens next. In this regard, the quality of television series that are exclusively streamed on a certain VSP is critical. This chapter provided a context of the rise of original productions on VSPs, with a case analysis of the "Mist Theater" suspense drama series on iQIYI. The production of original drama series is of strategic concern for the VSPs, especially with regard to their branding and differentiation. A critical concern of how some "blunt" advertisements interrupt the viewing experience of the television series on VSPs is raised as these VSPs are not relying on subscription fees alone, somewhat unlike Netflix.

One of the biggest differences between Netflix and Chinese VSPs is the technological affordance of *Danmaku*, or the "bullet screen," which allows real-time comments from viewers to cross the screen in a bullet-like movement. The range of bullet-screened topics and how the bullet screen affects the viewing experience is of great interest. In Chapter 3, Xiaying Xu and Qingyuan Zhao analyzed bullet screen comments on *Crime Crackdown* (2021). With the help of Python, they captured bullet screen comments from the platform Tencent Video to identify any patterns throughout the show. Significant patterns in relation to different categories of bullet screen comments were identified. As random and fragmented as they may appear, bullet screening comments are somewhat predictable. How bullet screening affects the viewing experience of a suspense genre is the second focus of this chapter. One may wonder if the suspense will be spoiled or intensified by the bullet screen. It is also interesting to ponder how viewers help one another through space and (a)synchronously. This chapter also contributes to the area of audience studies and convergence culture as championed by Jenkins (2006) as it provides an account of bullet-screening: a new form of co-formation of the media landscape.

In Chapter 4, Wei Jiang and Pengcheng Zhou interviewed five seasoned practitioners to gain insights into a series of critical topics that concern the life and death of their profession. Both positive and negative impacts of a stricter taxation policy brought to the industry are discussed. Equally important to this chapter is the discussion of the 30-episode limit for TV drama productions. What does it mean to produce and consume when such a policy is at work? The interview is about how big data and artificial intelligence changes the ecosystem of the industry and provides fresh insight. Scriptwriters, the creative core of the industry, face tremendous challenges, if not irritation, from algorithms that give unprofessional market-oriented recommendations. That is one of the problems caused by an excess of data. On the other hand, the sales of some special genres, especially relatively new ones, may also be affected by a lack of data support. Is it possible to "let one hundred flowers blossom" if scriptwriting and TV drama production are intervened by big data? Will the lines be more natural to actors and actresses, or will they be stuttering? What is the relationship between the platform and production companies? Finally, how COVID-19 has impacted the industry is also briefly discussed.

We thank Anthem Press for their interest and enthusiasm for publishing this book on Chinese television. We would also like to thank Doctor Max Sexton for his initial advice and feedback on our manuscripts. Special thanks go to Professor Tony Schirato, who encouraged our attempts and made this book happen before he passed away in 2019.

References

CNNIC (China Internet Network Information Center) 2021, "The 49th Development Report of China's Internet". Available online at http://www.cnnic.cn/hlwfzyj/hlwxzbg/hlwtjbg/202202/P020220318335949959545.pdf

Curtin, M. 2009, "Matrix media". In Graeme Turner and Jinna Tay (eds), *Television Studies After TV*. New York: Routledge.

Fan, Z. & Chen, X. (eds) 2021, *Blue Book of China TV Series 2021*. Beijing: Peking University Press.

Fung, A. 2009, "Globalizing televised culture: the case of China". In Graeme Turner and Jinna Tay (eds), *Television Studies After TV*. New York: Routledge.

Hidalgo, M. T., Segarra, S. J., & Palomares, S. P. 2021, "In-depth study of Netflix's original content of fictional series. Forms, styles and trends in the new streaming scene". *Communication & Society*, Vol. 34, No. 3, pp. 1–13.

Merriam-webster.com 2022, "Webisode". https://www.merriam-webster.com/dictionary/webisode

Raats, T. & Evans, T. 2021, ""If you can't beat them, be them" A critical analysis of the local streaming platform and Netflix alternative Streamz". *MediaKultur*, No. 70, pp. 50–65.

Wang, W. Y. & Lobato, R. 2009, "Chinese video streaming services in the context of global platform studies", *Chinese Journal of Communication*, Vol. 12, No. 3, pp. 365–371.
Jenkins, H. 2006, *Convergence Culture: Where Old and New Media Collide*. New York: New York University Press.
Wikipedia 2022, *Webisode*. https://en.wikipedia.org/wiki/Webisode
Zhao, Y. 1998, *Media, Market and Democracy in China, Between the Party Line and the Bottom Line*. Urbana-Champaign, IL: University of Illinois Press.

Chapter 1

WEBISODE DISTRIBUTION AND GLOBALIZATION STRATEGIES OF VIDEO-STREAMING PLATFORMS: TAKING iQIYI AS AN EXAMPLE

Zhixia Mo and Hui Liu

Introduction

Set up in 2010, iQIYI was famous for its technical innovation and creative video content and was merged with Baidu Company in 2013. Listed on NASDAQ in 2018, iQIYI leads the market and has claimed to be China's Netflix (Pham 2018).

Webisodes, with a few new features in content, platforms and technology, shape a new ecology of online distribution. Initially, the content of video-streaming platforms (VSPs) came from purchased copyright, which became increasingly expensive, so VSPs turned to produce originals to attract subscribers.[1]

With its large popularity, China is a potential VSP(s) market. However, due to state censorship, Netflix has not made its way into the Chinese mainland, so the Chinese market is shared by local VSPs, including iQIYI, Tencent Video and Youku.

Among these online video platforms, iQIYI leads the group by originals and also reflects how innovative strategies have shaped the ecology of Chinese VSP(s).

---

1 The originals, a kind of online TV series, can be classified into several types in the perspective of production methods, self-made originals, Intellectual Property (IP) purchase originals and co-produced originals. Self-made originals indicate that both scripts and production are from the same producer. IP purchase originals mean scripts are from another medium, such as novels or films, in which producers could recompose the plots. Regarding co-produced originals, producers consist of several corporations and divide works together.

The popularity of iQIYI started with originals, which were similar to Netflix's *House of Cards* (2010). The 12-episode drama *Time Raiders*(2015), co-produced by iQIYI and Huanrui Century Union (with 5 million CNY for each episode), was launched, and members could get a sneak peek of the webisode (iQIYI Inc 2020). This resulted in a craze for viewing and explosive growth in paid users. By the end of 2015, iQIYI's paid members had hit 10 million for the first time (Frater 2020).

Therefore, focusing on iQIYI, we discuss the features of original creations and how they constructed basic laws for the creation of the VSP(s). In this way, we provide an indication of the innovation of VSP(s) in China, which greatly influenced the TV industry.

Besides, iQIYI has applied many audience strategies to improve the audience's loyalty. With combined membership interest, iQIYI is trying to improve audience interest in renewing their subscription. Cooperating with TV terminals, iQIYI has extended its platform to access more audiences. By technology application, iQIYI, powered by Baidu, analyzes user information, bringing interesting content to satisfy the viewing experience.

So, it is worthwhile to discuss what are the audience strategies of iQIYI so that we can know how VSP(s) thoroughly attract their audience.

In addition, VSPs have been seeking outward expansion in their development. iQIYI prefers creations with Chinese characteristics in the global market. For example, iQIYI internationalized its content and entered the Asia market in cooperation with Netflix and Sony. Also, iQIYI has exploited the Malaysian market and expanded through VSP, including North America, Singapore, South Korea and Japan (Vena 2019), as the global audience is increasingly interested in Chinese-language programs.

The case indicated how online distribution of webisodes boosted the popularity of VSPs and increased its market scale, leading to a revolution in TV series viewing and changing the ecology of TV distribution.

To conclude, online distribution has changed traditional television distribution methods and brought new features for TV broadcasts. Through the case study, this chapter analyses the features of iQIYI, including platform growth, original production and audience strategies that have constructed a Chinese model of VSP(s) to explain the distribution methods and tendencies of TV series on VSPs. Lastly, the chapter probes into the globalization strategies of VSPs and analyzes iQIYI's features in international competition with originals with Chinese characteristics.

Understanding the Chinese model of VSP(s) would provide insight into how VSP(s) explore its path to expand the audience market in china and the globe, as a reference to further development.

Ecology of Video-Streaming Platforms

Streaming media build their online platforms where they broadcast videos, purchase copyrighted content from TV channels, and then produce original TV series. Netflix's growth experience shows how VSPs stand out with excellent original series. In China, VSPs have been developing for nearly 18 years. At first, the good and the bad were intermingled in the industry. Through establishing regulatory systems, financial crises and mergers and acquisitions (M&As), professional VSPs have taken shape. The current stage sees a tripartite confrontation of iQIYI, Youku and Tencent Video, with a cohort of rising short-video platforms. From iQIYI's experience, we can review the development of Chinese professional video websites in a nutshell.

Chronology of Chinese streaming media: From decentralized development to industry integration

There has been an integrated trend in Chinese streaming media over the past 20 years. Companies developed online video businesses and experienced (M&As). Finally, the three giant companies, Youku Tudou (Alibaba), Tencent Video (Tencent) and iQIYI (Baidu), formed a main pattern for the Chinese streaming video industries. This also means main production resources and creative innovation would happen within these giant companies, and their working models are presenting a trend that china's VSP(s) are driven by advanced technologies of internet industries.

Before 2004, although video services were available on the internet, there were no professional video websites. It was not until November 2004 that LeTV became China's first professional streaming video website. In the first half of 2005, Tudou.com, 56.com, Joy.cn, PPTV and PPS were launched one after another.

During this period, VSPs had different positioning strategies. LeTV was positioned as a long video website specializing in film and TV distribution. Tudou.com, 56.com and Joy.cn were regarded as video-sharing websites relying on user uploads. PPS and PPTV were network TV clients supported by a P2P technology.

The year 2006 witnessed explosive growth in video websites when Youku, Ku6.com, 6 Rooms, Baomihua.com, StormPlayer, PPlive, PPS and other influential websites were born and grew up. Additionally, some portals, including Sohu, Sina and Netease, attempted to enter the video industry.

The growth of the network video industry accelerated in 2008. But restricted by national regulatory administrations, dozens of video websites were shut down and penalized per *Administrative Regulations on Internet*

Audio-Visual Program Services. (State Broadcasting, Film & TV Administration, 2007) Additionally, the financial crisis affected more than 400 video websites, most of which had to downsize.

Between 2009 and 2011, central-level media engaged in VSP and competed with commercial streaming services. At the end of 2009, China Central Television (CCTV) launched CNTV—its network version. Subsequently, media groups set up their network TV channels to enrich the state-owned assets of video websites. As new blood, state-owned network TV channels were endowed with advantages, including policy support, orthodox content and advertising resources. However, they failed to grow quickly, lacking survival pressure, user awareness and innovation. Compared with the other two opponents, state-owned network TV channels were disadvantageous in web traffic and user loyalty.

In 2010, Baidu established iQIYI to develop copyrighted HD long online videos, while other VSPs started financing. In August 2010, LeTV was listed on the Growth Enterprise Market of the Shenzhen Stock Exchange and was funded with 730 million CNY (Cao 2020). In December 2010, Youku became a listed company on the NYSE, raising 203 million USD, and in May 2011, the corporate-issued additional shares were worth 593 million USD. In February 2011, PPLive received an investment totalling 250 million USD from SoftBank. In August 2011, Tudou went public on the NASDAQ and raised 174 million USD (Custer 2011). Later, multiple VSPs were founded successively. In the same year (2011), Tencent Video was established; in 2012, Mango TV; and in 2014, Migu Video and Fusion. By 2014, China's network video industry market had been shared by the state-owned network televisions, portals and commercial video websites.

From 2012 to 2013, VSPs saw a tide of M&As and entered a steady phase. After years of development and market restructuring, the network video industry became increasingly mature. Numerous enterprises were listed, merged and acquired, which facilitated the industry to develop in an all-around way.

The merger between Youku and Tudou.com and the one between iQIYI and PPS signified industry integration. Firstly, Youku joined hands with Tudou.com—China's earliest and most influential network video platform, established in April 2005. Tudou.com used to be among the first-tiered players in the Chinese video industry. In 2012, the company claimed a merger with Youku. Secondly, iQIYI merged with PPS. Claiming a profit in 2009, PPS used to dominate video websites and receive venture capital. Nevertheless, since the video industry was demanding capital flow and there were no deep pockets, PPS failed in IPOs and could do nothing but struggle with its second-tiered competitors. On May 7, 2013, Baidu announced spending 370 million USD on PPS's video business (100 percent shareholding) and merged the business with its independent video producer iQIYI (Baidu Inc 2020).

China's network video industry has seen rapid growth and booming business. With the participation of Baidu, Alibaba and Tencent (hereafter referred to as BAT), the whole industry is shared by Youku Tudou (Alibaba), Tencent Video (Tencent) and iQIYI (Baidu).

The development of Internet companies has driven the VSP(s) to become technology-oriented platforms, which enables the VSP(s) laid technological foundation and gets investment resource. Therefore VSP(s) got enough funding for their expansion through China. Also, the VSP(s) formed an intimate cooperation with the Internet companies, enabling them to make use of the advantage of internet technology.

Chronology of iQIYI: A cyclical effect driven by membership payment and originals

Membership payment and originals are key factors in how iQIYI gathers audiences to its platforms and makes audiences trust the platforms so that the VSP(s) gradually develop its own audience base and generate money flow by membership mechanism.

The development of iQIYI can be categorized into three stages in its creation strategies. It also implied how iQIYI explored creation style with their own characteristics as well as presented its ambition to be the largest VSP(s) in China. From copyrighted films to originals, iQIYI never stopped to expand its film library, which is also the main attraction to the audiences.

From 2013 to 2015, Stage 1 was a period driven by copyrighted films. Many movies were launched without a window period to attract customers. In this way, iQIYI's members exceeded 5 million, which laid the foundation for the company's businesses. Stage 2 is between 2015 and 2017, when iQIYI's members had gone up to 20 million. Regarded as the starting year of webisodes, 2015 saw the debut of membership payment.

In 2015, a Chinese novel about a tomb robbery named *Time Raiders*(2015) was adapted into a webisode of the same name, which was available for paid viewers. Within five minutes after episodes 5–12 were released simultaneously, the requests for the play hit 160 million times, and the requests for membership payment exceeded 2.6 million times (China News 2015). iQIYI's server crashed due to excessive visits and did not recover until the next day after all-night restoration. The *Time Raiders*(2015) brought a surge in paid members, which enabled iQIYI to expand its paid member base to 10 million for the first time.

Since Chinese users were used to watching free videos, iQIYI lacked confidence in membership payment at first, thus offering users several free episodes to raise their interest. When audiences indulged in the series, a pop-up emerged, persuading them to spend ¥19.8/month or ¥43/quarter on a VIP membership with which they could enjoy ads removal and sneak peek. Such a strategy was so effective that by June 16, 2015, iQIYI's VIP members had exceeded 5 million (Tao, 2015).

iQIYI continued its victorious pursuit by developing user payment. On July 2, 2015, iQIYI agreed with Paramount Pictures on a film library that covered 800 finished films and other upcoming productions (Niu 2015). On July 8, 2015, the press release of the Hong Kong popular singer Eason Chan's new album was broadcast to iQIYI members. On July 10, 2015, iQIYI broadened its sales channels of VIP membership cards by vending the first batch of physical cards in 7-Eleven stores. On July 24, 2015, iQIYI built a diverse VIP member movie bank, and several online blockbusters got traffic of more than 10 million visitors (Tao, 2015).

On February 24, 2016, *Descendants of the Sun*(2016), the first TV series simultaneously available in China and South Korea, was exclusively launched on iQIYI, with an overall 400 million views of the first four episodes. iQIYI members could watch the series simultaneously as those in South Korea did, while non-members had to wait for a week. The popularity of *Descendants of the Sun*(2016) among netizens boosted the population of iQIYI members. Gong Yuxuan, founder of iQIYI, claimed 20 million iQIYI members in June 2016, 30 million by 2016 and 50.8 million by 2017. Member revenue was also on the rise. Between 2015 and 2017, the yearly figures reached 996.7 million CNY, 3.8 billion CNY and 6.5 billion CNY, which accounted for 18.7 percent, 33.5 percent and 37.6 percent of the total revenue, respectively. Membership had become the second major source of profit apart from advertising. From 2015 to 2017, iQIYI's investment in content registered 3.7 billion CNY, 7.5 billion CNY and 12.6 billion CNY, which accounted for 61 percent, 67 percent and 73 percent of the total cost, respectively. (iQIYI Inc 2017)

In this stage, iQIYI had spent a large amount of investment on cooperation with content companies to get popular webisode resources, attracting audiences and cultivating their viewing habits. It could be seen as a form that cultivates audiences' paying habits for the membership, therefore expanding iQIYI's membership scale for future growth.

Stage 3 is from 2017 to the present, with originals as the driving force. There are various originals, such as webisodes and variety shows. Webisodes include *Tientsin Mystic*(2017), *Burning Ice*(2017) and *Story of Yanxi Palace*(2018), while variety shows: *The Rap of China*(2017), *Idol Producer*(2018) and *The Big Band*(2019).

In 2018, iQIYI launched dozens of exclusive webisodes. Thanks to the originals, iQIYI members had exceeded 100 million by June 2019 (iQIYI Inc 2019a). iQIYI's success in membership not only increases its revenue but also boosts its confidence in purchasing or creating quality content, with which the platform can enhance its influence, attract new users and meet the expectations of ad clients. This helps raise the conversion rate of paid members and build a virtuous cycle between ads and membership. Alongside Baidu's AI technology, iQIYI can better understand user preferences and push suitable content to maintain their online duration, similar strategy by Netflix.

At this stage, iQIYI's creations expressed a trend that it met the needs of young audiences, and the advantage of original production brought a solid foundation of the audience to the platform.

Creation Law for Video-Streaming Platforms

To satisfy audiences' demand, streaming media need a broad video source. Usually, VSPs' content comes from brand cooperation, copyright purchase and original production. Although these methods could expand VSPs' broadcast resources, there are also risks. For instance, streaming media spend money on episodes but are suddenly required to pay higher copyright loyalty and even change or terminate the contract. This will put VSPs in a passive position. Therefore, it is necessary to value original production so as to take the initiative in content and control the whole industry chain in creation, distribution and showing.

As the pioneering VSPs in China, iQIYI underlines original investment and production. Nowadays, iQIYI underscores developing premium-quality content and cooperates closely with third-party creators. At the preliminary stage, iQIYI was a streaming platform inexperienced in creation that used to partner with seasoned producers and TV channels. Later, the company explored and cooperated with professional online video agencies and studios to build creation groups. Besides, iQIYI also encouraged user creation by supporting users to release their quality creations on its platform. To continuously attract users, iQIYI followed the "exclusive broadcast and self-production strategy." iQIYI purchased exclusive copyright and created its segmented market, which differed from other Chinese VSPs.

Afterward, original series have become vitally important in the content strategy of streaming media, and their genres have been enriched. iQIYI has not yet bred a reputed team at a stage where the Chinese film and TV industry is still developing. Thus, it is uncommon for a single creation group to release several works. iQIYI attempts to produce its original series. Normally, Chinese webisodes are based on online novel adaptations, Intellectual Property (hereafter referred to as IP) sequels and genre-based series. Since 2011, video websites have taken shape and itched for film and TV production. Implementing the self-production strategy, iQIYI launched its first webisode, *Say Yes Online*(2011). In 2014, *The Ferry Man*() made its first screen appearance. The webisode reflected reality with its quirky plot and became a phenomenon followed by sequels in the next three consecutive years. iQIYI also rearranged the Chinese online novels into new IPs as crucial topics. In June 2015, the self-produced webisode *Time Raiders*(2015), adapted from the novel of the same name, was broadcast, where iQIYI first introduced a member sneak peek. Within 25 days, the views amounted to 100 million (Tao, 2015). From then on, iQIYI released other high-grade IP adaptations such as *The Mystic Nine*(2016), *Tientsin Mystic*(2017), *Guilty of Mind*(2017) and *With You* (2016).

Since then, as the series quality improved, iQIYI further developed genre-based series and explored niche genres. The reputed webisodes *Legend of Yun Xi*(2018) and *The Thunder* were the first broadcast online and then on TV. Also, iQIYI started to produce different genre-based series, such as *The Thunder*(2019), an adaptation from a real criminal case in China; *Sword Dynasty*(2019), a Chinese Kungfu drama; and *Winter Begonia*(2020), a love story in the Republic of China. These non-mainstream productions took in the style of traditional Chinese culture or China's actual conditions. They got rid of the inherent focus in a certain genre by integrating character design with the series features *My Roommate is a Detective*(2020); the character personalities penetrated the comedic elements through intense and exciting detection, which combined suspense, inference and comedy. iQIYI's original webisodes coincided with the internet vogue and broke through the suspense stereotype.

Besides, content with good quality is another strategy for iQIYI to improve. Although iQIYI has made efforts to improve content quality and word of mouth, there is still room to improve its production quality, especially compared to a video produced by worldwide streaming platforms, such as Netflix.

In the early years, iQIYI produced different genre-based series in internet style with modest quality. After years of experience accumulation, iQIYI came to realize that self-produced webisodes can meet audience demand and launched youth-based webisodes, including *With You*(2016), *My Huckleberry Friends*(2017), *Somewhere Only We Know*(2019) and *Legend of Yun Xi*(2018), as well as suspense webisodes including *Burning Ice*(2017), *Original Sin*(2018), *Detective Chinatown*(2020) and *The Listener*(2019). However, even though the series became popular, the overall rating on word of mouth could be lower when compared with Netflix.

To further analyze the quality of the product of iQIYI, it is better to evaluate from the audience's perspective. The sheet below compares the evaluation records of 10 top-rating paid webisodes from Netflix and iQIYI in the 2017 Douban Rating, respectively (in no particular order).

iQIYI		Netflix	
My Huckleberry Friends(2017)	8.6	*The Get Down*(2016)	9.3
Tientsin Mystic(2017)	8.2	*Sense8*(2015)	9.1
Legal Mavericks(2017)	7.7	*Master of None*(2015)	8.9
Burning Ice(2017)	8.2	*Annie*(2017)	8.8
The Hunting Genius(2017)	6.9	*Orange Is the New Black*(2013)	8.9
Nirvana in Fire 2(2017)	8.5	*Mindhunter*(2017)	8.9
Stardom(2016)	4.6	*Dark*(2017)	8.6
Undercover(2017)	6.3	*Stranger Things*(2016)	8.8
Candle in the Tomb: Mu Ye Gui Shi(2017)	3.0	*Atypical*(2017)	8.5
Infernal Affairs(2017)	6.3	*Unbreakable Kimmy Schmidt*(2015)	8.6
Average	6.83	Average	8.84

Data Source: Douban / https://movie.douban.com

According to the above ratings of the top 10 originals launched in the same year by Netflix and iQIYI, the average score of Netflix webisodes is 8.84, which is far higher than that of iQIYI webisodes in the same period. Moreover, Netflix originals are comparable, indicating relatively high-quality production on average. Despite top productions such as *Tientsin Mystic*(2017), iQIYI's webisodes are on various levels, which implies room for general quality improvement.

As audiences raise their aesthetic demands, VSPs lift the standards for self-produced webisodes accordingly. VSPs emphasized content quality and attracted users with exclusive productions. Streaming media work with renowned and powerful creators to guarantee the quality of content creation. Only when the content is refined can it bring continuous surprises to audiences and maintain their trust in the platform, therefore realizing stable growth in the subscription. Besides, streaming media focus on production and broadcast as televisions do. But their broadcast accessibility and content style differ from traditional televisions. This facilitates streaming media to cash their content on the internet more flexibly.

Audience Strategy of Video-Streaming Platforms

According to the methods that iQIYI provides, we can know the rules of audience management to satisfy audiences' needs.

Implementing user-oriented membership strategies

IQIYI strives to improve user experience and raise the subscription rate by implementing more specific comprehensive strategies.

First, making full use of premium-quality content, iQIYI develops a whole-industry chain. By building a content-based ecosystem of digital entertainment that integrates industries such as gaming, literature, movies and e-commerce, iQIYI developed an "Apple Tree" model. This business model provides several vertical businesses operated in the form of ads or membership that may vary accordingly. Finally, the enterprise satisfies multiple user demands on culture and entertainment.

To further enhance the platform's audience base, iQIYI took measures to retain audiences' subscription rates and cultivates user interest in paid viewing.

IQIYI, along with other Chinese internet companies, offers co-branded membership discounts to increase customers' interest. For example, iQIYI announced shared membership with Ctrip, a leading player in online booking in the tourism industry in China. Members who purchase iQIYI Diamond VIP or QIYIGUO year card benefits on the iQIYI platform can claim the benefits of Ctrip Prime members. Similarly, customers who become Ctrip Prime members can activate an eight-month VIP membership on iQIYI. Ctrip once granted iQIYI V7 VIP members (there are seven levels of iQIYI VIP members, from V1 to V7) with all the perks at no extra cost, including the use of Ctrip's VIP airport lounges, priority access for purchasing train tickets, no-hassle cancellation on hotel bookings within China. The exercise rate for VIP airport lounges was as high as 43 percent (Inc 2019a).

Similar strategies were applied after the first try of cooperation on membership. IQIYI launched a joint membership program with JD.com, a major online shopping platform in China, which attracted over one million users in the first week (Inc 2018b). The special offers from JD.com and iQIYI included but were not limited to shopping. The rights and interests of membership covered every aspect of people's life, popularizing value-added services and cross-border rights and interests.

In this way, the crossover between the giants in e-commerce and video content attracted more customers due to their business and brand values. Even consumers would get discounts from both platforms. With a consumption upgrade, more users pay for quality content and services. These users are highly overlapped in entertainment and e-commerce. Furthermore, the cooperation above represents the business trend of new retailing, that is, the blend of e-commerce and pan-entertainment.

However, iQIYI is facing some challenges. Notwithstanding the attractive joint membership, it was the initial action to expand its membership for a period of time. There was slow growth on the platform afterward. By the end of the second quarter of 2022, iQIYI's total membership was 98.3 million, reduced to 900,000 from the year before. The data indicated that the growth rate had slowed down.

In addition, other factors also influence the decrease in membership subscriptions. Inadequate supervision under the safety of account usage led to shared subscription accounts, where people would reduce their costs on subscriptions. With the impacts of the post-pandemic, a group of Chinese people tends to reduce their entertainment spending since they face personal financial burdens. Some people will give up renewing their subscription when the platform increases its subscription fee.

To keep the audience's loyalty to a specific platform, it is not enough to enjoy china's demographic dividend and increasing acceptance rate on a payment plan in the country. As for iQIYI, preferential policies are applied to encourage users to renew their subscriptions, such as reducing the audience's cost if they renew the account.

Cooperating with terminals to enter the TV industry

To enter the TV industry, it is pivotal for VSPs to cooperate with hardware terminals in a content broadcast. iQIYI collaborates with several terminals. For example, iQIYI worked with Galaxy Internet Television to provide the Qiyiguo TV app, allowing users to watch the content of iQIYI on a smart TV (QiyiguoTV 2018). Qiyiguo TV does not share the membership with iQIYI unless users pay for the permit. With the permit, the membership can be available on mobile, computer, iPad and TV.

In addition, iQIYI also designs smart set-top boxes (hereafter referred to as STB(s)) and develops home theater systems. iQIYI joined forces with Baidu and BGCTV to launch a new-gen AI-integrated STB named "Gehua Little Fruit Set Top Box"(iQIYI Inc 2018a). The STB adds intelligent functions to television by integrating the traditional cable TV network broadcast with internet VOD to provide at-home video entertainment. With integrated plans, a differentiated price system and diversified pathways of profit-making, the co-invention helped the three parties realize mutual benefits and a win-win situation.

As a whole, iQIYI engages in hardware terminals. It fully develops member subscriptions and transmits content via multiple terminals to satisfy members' viewing demand in an all-around way. Thanks to Baidu's hardware and internet technology, iQIYI has successfully invented its STB. This indicates that VSPs are multi-channelled since they rely on users and enter various industries, greatly impacting the traditional digital television industry.

Improving creation capacity and broadcast efficiency with AI

Apart from content, technology is also crucial for VSP operation. With technological innovation, content can be fully explored.

Firstly, AI helps collect user data, analyze users' viewing demand and make intelligent recommendations to audiences. iQIYI uses AI to raise its creation efficiency and fully realizes AI-assisted content creation and operation. "The most prominent difference between iQIYI and traditional entertainment services is that the former is driven by not only content creation but also technological innovation." said Gong Yu, founder of iQIYI (Zhang,2017). For iQIYI, AI has become the infrastructure of content creation, user insights and content distribution, including scripting, casting, traffic prediction, review, coding, editing, operation, searching, recommendation, publicity, hotspot prediction and extraction, idol chasing, advertising campaigns and online customer services. Take iQIYI Aichuang Media System as an example. iQIYI has initiated a new film and TV production solution, integrating software, hardware and network. The solution conducts an AI analysis on photographed materials to realize high-efficiency film and TV production. The system was applied to iQIYI's large-scale reality shows *The Rap of China*(2018), *Idol Hits*(2018), *The Chinese Youth*(2018) and *Idol Producer: Season 2*(2020). It has changed the traditional post-production process and improved the efficiency of content creation, thus reforming the process in film and TV production.

Besides, AI and big data can precisely analyze user profiles. iQIYI uses AI to endow itself with imagination in creation. In accordance with viewer demand, AI can predict the viewing effect and give insightful suggestions on creation. iQIYI has developed an intelligent casting system—Yihui. The system accurately matches producers with artists with natural language processing and AI. Yihui has nominated Zhang Xueying as the actress in the webisode *Summer's Desire* (2018) and Liu Haoran, the actor in *With You* (2016), both of whom have been well received. At present, producing original webisodes needs strong financial support. Owing to AI technology, increasing originals can effectively cut costs on content. Regarding webisode traffic, the accuracy of the 1-year and 0.5-year predictions are as high as 88 percent. This means that AI helps iQIYI achieve high-cost performance and appropriate copyright purchase and predict and create more potentially popular content. In addition, *Reduzhi* (热度值, popularity value) can provide integrated services. The indicator analyzes user viewing, interaction and sharing data and sets science-based standards for content to select and recommend webisodes. In this way, iQIYI can offer a better consumption experience and higher content value to users, producers and business partners. AI further enhances the VSPs' business capacity. iQIYI's AI identification correlates ads with content, strengthening the enterprise's monetization capacity. The 2018 summer blockbuster *Story of Yanxi Palace*(2018) has attracted wide public attention, with over 12.8 billion post views and over 9.97 discussion times on Weibo (Covosphere 2018). Moreover, contextual advertising has gained good feedback. AI identifies characters, plots, behaviors, actions, emotions and lines, improving advertising campaigns and user experience.

In the future, technology updates will further increase VSP subscribers. 5G has realized high speed and low latency, leaving more space for iQIYI technology. According to the interview with iQIYI technologists, in the 5G era, VR will improve user experience in new consumption scenarios. Content consumption will be deepened, and AI-integrated VR and AR can develop more scenarios. Besides, VR can combine content, hardware and interactive games.

Moreover, in the 5G era, iQIYI aims to expand the entertainment scenario through sound and video technology, including increasing the input in HDR. Also, audiences have a higher demand for definition and sound, expecting a better viewing experience. Currently, Blu-ray, Dolby Version and 1080p resolution are popular. In future years, 5G will enhance the definition and sound quality. "Users pursue better experience. We perfect their consumption experience with sustainable premium-quality content. When 5G is widely used, 4K and 8K will be mainstream, and that's an irreversible trend," mentioned Yang in an interview (He 2019).

AI expands the creative space for VSPs and improves their entertainment quality. It is influencing VSPs' content production, insight into user demand and content distribution in an all-around, in-depth way. This signifies that VSPs cannot develop without technology. AI's deepened development and application will enhance VSPs' user awareness, urging them to serve audiences with better entertainment services. This will influence the future entertainment ecology.

iQIYI's Globalization Strategies

In recent years, Chinese VSPs represented by iQIYI have expanded overseas. iQIYI authorizes original overseas series, but its overseas expansion rate is still slow.

iQIYI has been exporting its first-rating originals that are recognized by an increasing amount of large international entertainment copyright purchasers. Several sensational webisodes, such as *The Mystic Nine*(2016) and *With You*(2016), have been distributed overseas. Since 2017, iQIYI has created several quality webisodes, including *Tientsin Mystic*(2017) and *Burning Ice*(2017), which meet the production standards for the American series and have cinematic textures. They not only have earned a good reputation and web traffic among Chinese viewers but also have influenced the international market. As a word-of-mouth masterpiece by iQIYI, *Tientsin Mystic*(2017) has been broadcast on Netflix and three major TV channels in Hong Kong/Macau, Malaysia/Brunei and Singapore, namely, TVB, Astro, and StarHub (Hawkes 2017). *Tientsin Mystic*(2017) and *Burning Ice*(2017) were distributed exclusively in Taiwan via iQIYI Taiwan. *Burning Ice*(2017) was launched simultaneously in Hong Kong and the Chinese mainland and distributed to Southeast Asia, Japan, South Korea, North America, Europe and other foreign territories, among which the distribution right in Southeast Asia belongs to Netflix.

In 2019, iQIYI claimed its globalization strategies by introducing the iQIYI app worldwide. The company has prioritized the Southeast Asia market and built a strategic partnership with the Malaysian media Astro. Astro can be benefited from iQIYI's operation via the latter's technological products and content creation platform, while iQIYI can access local users through Astro's media and marketing networks. Malaysians can either log in iQIYI app with an Astro account or enjoy iQIYI entertainment services by registering a new one with their emails, Facebook or Google accounts (IQIYI Inc 2020). Statistics have shown that, Chinese operators are ranked top in-app quantity and castability in Malaysia.

iQIYI has entered 14 countries and regions by far. When concluding the company's overseas experience, Gong likened the Chinese cultural products and services to "the dowry": "In the past, Chinese content had to be distributed abroad via destination channels. Otherwise, films launched in overseas cinemas would cover few audiences, resulting in low attendance. Likewise, without destination channels, TV series would find it hard to be broadcast on TV due to policy, economic and technological restrictions. Nonetheless, with the popularity of the internet, the world has been interconnected. Since internet software and services are customized with strong R&D, data storage and operating capacity, there is a high threshold for media in mid-and small-sized countries to export content. Under these circumstances, Chinese companies can export content bundled with technology" (Jiang,2019).

As iQIYI deepens its overseas expansion, it will face localization challenges, including languages, cultures, religions, networks and GDP per capita. In addition, it is necessary to consider the natives' viewing habits, interests and purchasing power in cross-cultural communication.

Currently, iQIYI is exporting its originals on overseas platforms. This showcases the glamour of Chinese content and lays a foundation for the firm's further overseas expansion. So, iQIYI needs to produce originals with Chinese characteristics and focus on the local interests in viewing. There are two categories of audiences for iQIYI: overseas Chinese and foreigners outside China. iQIYI needs to be crystal clear about the production style and audience positioning. It should carry forward its creations and integrate them with exotic cultures to expand the viewing market.

Conclusion and Discussion: Distribution Methods of Webisodes

This chapter concentrates on the development of VSPs. The authors have analyzed iQIYI and discussed the Chinese VSP's development strategies. iQIYI has accumulations in its business ecosystems, and its experience is valuable with its special business environment, user category, self-positioning and business strategy. In conclusion, the suggestions are as follows.

Firstly, valuing original creation and production to enhance VSPs' core competitiveness. VSPs offer more than viewing services, and content quality is their core competitiveness in attracting subscribers. Besides, considering the fierce contest among VSPs, it is essential to implement a differentiated strategy to find one's unique advantages over its rivals. In TV program creation, producers should consider universality and probe into differentiation.

Secondly, having user awareness and improving services with technology. In China, advertisements remain an indispensable method for VSPs to create income. At present, VSPs increasingly profit from subscriptions. With a population base in a specific area, subscription attracts users with rich video content, develops their habits to pay, raises user loyalty and encourages renewed payment to exploit a blue sea. Joint membership characterizes iQIYI. In the future, users will be encouraged to pay regularly, and VSPs should further consider member personalities, subscription fees and member rights and interests. Also, big data and AI also back VSPs in user recommendation, preference prediction and advertising campaigns. Consequently, technology serves as strong, intelligent support for VSPs.

Thirdly, entering the TV industry and establishing a pan-entertainment platform. Grown in a network environment, VSPs break the tradition where film and TV developed separately and allow a symbiosis among various forms of art. iQIYI has engaged in different kinds of digital entertainment and established a pan-entertainment platform. Hence, VSPs should exert themselves to offer high-class and professional video content. It is worth noting that the streaming digital video system has changed traditional film and TV watching into online viewing. This is why we should consider how VSPs take advantage of differentiated viewing.

Fourthly, implementing globalization strategies to expand the business landscape. When VSPs have been rooted in a country or a region for a long, the market will be saturated, and the growth will slow down. In this situation, overseas users are a larger potential market. When developing into a certain scale, VSPs will seek overseas distribution and prepare for transnational expansion, during which they may tackle issues concerning multinational operations and cross-cultural communication. They have to collaborate with local enterprises to get authorization so natives can enjoy imported services. Later, VSPs should independently produce localized commercial videos that viewers understand, trust and are willing to pay for.

In the future, VSPs will prosper as before. But as their quantity grows, competition will be stiffer. Obviously, only VSPs with superior content and services can win user trust and sustainable subscriptions. Therefore, VSPs should center on user demand and readjust their development strategies to gear up for the ever-changing trend.

References

Baidu Inc.'Baidu Acquires Online Video Business of PPS for US $370 Million to Create China's Largest Online Video Platform | Baidu Inc'. 2020. Accessed December 4. https://ir.baidu.com/news-releases/news-release-details/baidu-acquires-online-video-business-pps-us-370-million-create/.

Cao, Minjie. 2020. 'Youku Refinances 400 Million USD after Half-Year Public Listing'. Accessed December 6. https://tech.qq.com/a/20110523/000047.htm.

Covosphere. 2018. 'Story of Yanxi Palace: Understanding Chinese Viewing Behaviour through Social Listening'. https://convosphere.com/story-of-yanxi-palace-understanding-chinese-viewing-behaviour-through-social-listening/.

Custer, C. 2011. 'Tudou Raises $174 Million in IPO'. https://www.techinasia.com/tudou-raises-174-million-in-ipo.

China News. 2015. 'The Script for the Second Season of "Time Raider" was Formed'. https://www.chinanews.com/yl/2015/07-16/7409811.shtml(In Chinese)

Frater, Patrick. 2020. 'China's IQIYI Claims 10 Million Paying Subscribers - Variety'. Accessed December 4. https://variety.com/2015/digital/asia/iqiyi-10-million-paying-subscribers-1201652618/#!

Hawkes, Rebecca. 2017. 'IQIYI Content Set for TVB, Astro, StarHub and Netflix | Deals | News'. *Rapid TV News*. https://www.rapidtvnews.com/2017120449943/iqiyi-content-set-for-tvb-astro-starhub-and-netflix.html#axzz6fO0qIlzU.

He. 2019. 'An In-Depth Report on IQIYI Membership Exceeding 100 Million: What Is the Next Step for Video Websites?' https://tech.sina.com.cn/i/2019-07-02/doc-ihytcerm0701864.shtml.

Tao,Wendong. 2015. 'IQIYI Has More Than 5 Million VIP Members'. https://m.huanqiu.com/article/9CaKrnJM7h4 (In Chinese).

iQIYI Inc. 2018a. 'IQIYI Joins Forces with Baidu and BGCTV to Launch Gehua Little Fruit Set Top Box'. https://www.prnewswire.com/news-releases/iqiyi-joins-forces-with-baidu-and-bgctv-to-launch-gehua-little-fruit-set-top-box-300720899.html.

———. 2018b. 'JD.Com and IQIYI Joint Membership Program Attracts a Combined One Million Users in the First Week.' https://www.prnewswire.com/news-releases/jdcom-and-iqiyi-joint-membership-program-attracts-a-combined-one-million-users-in-the-first-week-300645262.html.

———. 2019a. 'IQIYI and Ctrip Expand Strategic Cooperation in Shared Membership.' https://www.prnewswire.com/news-releases/iqiyi-and-ctrip-expand-strategic-cooperation-in-shared-membership-300783568.html.

iQIYI Inc. 2020. 'Members Can Enjoy a Sneak Peak of Time Raiders, an iQIYI Webisode Launched on June 12'. Accessed December 4 (In Chinese.) https://www.iq.yi.com/common/20150616/2c821ea6f7fc9e1f.html.

Jiang, Huizi. 2019. 'Gong Yu, CEO of IQiyi: China's Cultural Products Should Go Abroad with Dowry' https://baijiahao.baidu.com/s?id=1647988719222154917&wfr=spider&for=pc(In Chinese)

Niu, Yue. 2015. 'IQiyi Buys 800 Paramount Films|Business|chinadaily.Com.Cn'. https://usa.chinadaily.com.cn/us/2015-07/14/content_21281954.htm.

Pham, Sherisse. 2018. 'IQiyi, the Netflix of China, Is Going Public in the US.' 19. https://money.cnn.com/2018/02/28/technology/baidu-iqiyi-netflix-china/index.html.

QiyiguoTV. 2018. 'Qiyiguo TV: iQIYI's TV Terminal that Perfects Living Room Large-screen Film Watching Experience'. https://www.sohu.com/a/276682672_337865 (In Chinese).

State Broadcasting, Film & TV Administration. 2007. 'Film & TV Administration. Administrative Regulations on Internet Audio-Visual Program Service'. Order of the State Administration of Radio, Film, and Television and the Ministry of Information Industry No. 56. (In Chinese)

Tencent Inc. 2020. 'iQIYI CEO Gong Yu: Technology Facilitates Export of Chinese Cultural Content'. Accessed December 4. https://new.qq.com/omn/20191022/20191022A051SC00.html (In Chinese).

Vena, Danny. 2019. 'With 100 Million Subscribers in China, IQiyi Wants to Take Its Show on the Road'. https://www.fool.com/investing/2019/06/27/100-million-subscribers-iqiyi-expanding-abroad.aspx.

Zhang, Bei. 2017. 'Gong Yu, Founder and CEO of iQiyi, Attended The Baidu World Conference to Create a Big Entertainment Ecosystem with AI Technology'. http://m.techweb.com.cn/article/2017-11-16/2607084.shtml(In Chinese).

Zhang, Zongyi. 2020. 'How Netflix Expanded to 190 Countries in 7 Years'. Accessed November 30. https://hbr.org/2018/10/how-netflix-expanded-to-190-countries-in-7-years.

Chapter 2

THE PRODUCTION OF HIGH-QUALITY HOMEMADE SHORT DRAMAS ON CHINESE NETWORKS: THE EXAMPLE OF iQIYI'S MIST THEATER[1]

Jia Xian and Qinqin Ren

Introduction

As a new medium, the Internet has not only changed the one-way communication mode of traditional TV but also given birth to the new artistic form of self-produced dramas on the Internet; these productions are known as web-based self-produced dramas, but a clear definition has not yet been formed in the academic field. A network self-produced drama, as its name implies, is a film and television drama invested and shot by the network media itself, produced and broadcasted specifically for the network platform (Cao 2011, 113–116). It's also defined as an audiovisual art form that conforms to the law and characteristics of network communication, with network culture as the leading factor and Internet thinking as the driving force (Yang 2016, 37–39). Clearly, the definition of online self-made drama emphasizes the characteristics of video websites as the main body of production and the dissemination channel, as well as the media characteristics of the dissemination content.

With the prosperity of the UGC mode, online self-made dramas have developed (Feng 2016, 33). UGC represents User-Generated Content, and users access the network platform to create and disseminate personalized content. The emergence of websites such as YouTube in the United States

---

[1] This research is financially supported by the Chongqing Social Science Planning Project (重庆市社会科学规划项目), Research on Innovation and Strategies of Media Supervision Mechanism in Chongqing under the Background of Media Convergence (媒体融合背景下重庆传媒监管机制创新与对策研究). Research grant offered by Chongqing Office of Social Science Planning (重庆市社会科学规划办公室) (Project code:2022TBWT-ZD02).

has provided a platform for users to create and distribute personalized content. With the development of technology and the maturity of the UGC mode, many users began to develop into organized production groups with certain professional skills, and some professionals also began to participate in amateur creation (Ding 2014, 69–73), which promoted the transformation of online self-produced dramas from the UGC to PGC mode, that is, Professional-Generated Content. Video websites have flourished globally as professional content producers and distributors. Among them, Netflix in the United States adjusted its business model in 2007 against the backdrop of the rise in video sites, formally transforming from a DVD rental site to a streaming platform. With the premiere of *Lilyhammer* in 2012, Netflix became a producer of original content on par with HBO and other traditional pay TV stations (Osur 2016, 83). By continuously launching original boutique content and continuously attracting users to the platform, Netflix has become the video website with the largest number of paying users in the world.

In the domestic context, as one of the largest video sites in China, iQIYI launched the Mist Theater in the second quarter of 2020, which attracted widespread attention. It contains multiple short dramas of the same genre and volume, and achieves the pursuit of content quality by shortening the length of episodes and increasing the cost of single episode investment. At the same time, the use of genre theater has revolutionized the operation strategy and marketing model of video sites, thus amplifying the scale effect of high-quality short dramas and becoming an important means for video sites to build their brand image. In this sense, The Mist Theater also marks a new stage of development for self-produced dramas on the Internet.

Reviewing the development of web-based self-produced drama, since 2014, major video websites have stepped up efforts to make their own content and adopted differentiated competition, and the creative forms of online self-made dramas have been continuously differentiated (Wu & Du 2015, 188–192), this year is known as "the first year of content self-production in the Internet video industry." This chapter divides the development of online self-made dramas into the following three phases: a growth period (2014–2016), a period of exploration (2017–2020) and a period of development (since 2020).

During the growth period, video websites increased their investment in self-made content, and the year-on-year growth rate of online self-made dramas was as high as 192 percent (ENdata 2016, 6). Many suspense dramas, such as *The Death Notice* (2014) and *Soul Ferry* (2014), have attracted attention on the Internet.

In 2017, online self-produced dramas entered the second phase, a period of exploration, and China introduced a number of policies, such as the

"Broadband Restriction Order" and "Foreign Restriction Order," that had a huge impact on content production and the production of domestic dramas. Following this, the online drama market gradually returned to rationality, with the number of self-productions declining significantly as shown in the report of TV series industry development (2018, 5), and video sites began turning to the differentiated competition strategy of Content First. However, for domestic dramas, the length of a drama series determines the commercial profit and audience market to a certain extent: the more you sell, the more you earn. There are many phenomena, such as artificially lengthening the plot and slowing the narrative rhythm, that are used to increase dramatic capacity. The problem of "water injection dramas," that is, dramas with long and drawn-out plots, makes online homemade dramas, and even the TV drama industry, targets of criticism.

In February 2020, in response to the phenomenon of the watering down of TV and online dramas, National Radio and Television Administration (NRTA) issued "Regulations on Watering Down TV Dramas and Online Dramas," encouraging the creation of short dramas that are completed within 30 episodes. This measure not only corrects and adjusts for the previous long dramas but also marks the new phase of online self-made dramas. In May 2020, to respond to the government's call and promote the development of the platform, Tencent Video, iQIYI and Youku, together with six major production companies, issued the "Initiative on Uniting as One to Overcome the Difficulties of the Industry Self-Help Action" proposing to standardize episode lengths and promote the creation of fine short dramas.

Under the dual drive of policy guidance and industry development, online self-made dramas have transitioned to a short and high-quality development period. Various video websites have broadcast online self-made short dramas with different types and themes, with the number of episodes ranging from 12 to 24. These include *If There Is No Tomorrow* (2020) and *Detective Chinatown* (2020), which have aroused widespread concern in the domestic market with short and concise storylines and compact narratives. Since then, iQIYI's Mist Theater and Youku's Suspense Theater have been launched. The former, with 12 episodes as its creative volume, has launched a number of high-quality, short suspense dramas, which promotes the development of the genre of online self-made dramas and lays a solid foundation for the construction of the platform's brand image.

In this chapter, we explore the example of iQIYI's Mist Theater, which best represents the trend of high-quality short dramas. The author summarizes and refines the upgrading of its production level and creative techniques and the innovation of narrative mode and audiovisual language to inspire follow-up script creation. The production strategy and creative gains and losses of the short drama and high-quality theatrical content are also discussed, providing references for the future development of Chinese video streaming platforms.

The Development of Internet Self-made Short Dramas and the Birth of Mist Theater

Traditionally, the US television season is divided into off-season and peak season, with peak season generally running from September to April or May of the following year. During this period, traditional television stations attract viewers by filming weekly broadcasts on the side. Excluding some specific programming, a TV series in an acting season is generally about 25 episodes (Liao & Wu 2009, 44–47), and the off-season is filled with reruns or other programs. With the rise of pay TV, capturing the dozen weeks of the off-season market is an important means of differentiation. In this context, HBO launched quality short series under the slogan "Quality TV," and the collective volume of its series was not only adjusted to accommodate the off season but also laid the foundation for the improvement of production quality. This has become an important feature of the US drama model, has been continued in the production of streaming content and has also become an important reference for domestic video sites.

As early as the first stage of the development of domestic online dramas, short online dramas appeared that were characterized by the short length of a single episode, generally 5–15 minutes, with each episode telling a story independently (Zhou 2016, 8). This reflected the characteristics of a fragmented network and fast rhythm, and matched the audience's habits. In contrast, the current online self-made short dramas are not measured by the length of a single episode. As mentioned above, online self-made short dramas are relative to domestic long dramas. In the existing market since 2020, various video websites have launched short dramas with different themes and types, with the number of episodes ranging from 12 episodes to 22 episodes (Yang 2020, 91–94). The volume of short dramas not only conforms to the media characteristics of the network but also favored more by the capital market than are long dramas in terms of production investment.

The rise of online self-made skits is the result of the joint action of various forces. In 2008, NRTA issued the "Regulations on the Administration of Internet Audio-Visual Programs," which became the main legal basis for the management of Internet audiovisual programs. In 2017, it issued the "Notice on Several Policies to Support the Prosperity and Development of TV Plays," encouraging excellent TV drama production institutions to actively participate in the production of online dramas, which is of great significance to the improvement of the overall creation level of online dramas, and reflects the trend of specialization and quality of online homemade dramas. In 2020, NRTA's "Notice on Further Strengthening the Production and Management of TV Drama Creation" against water injection dramas once again highlighted the importance of content quality and film and television products, and pushed the development of online self-made dramas toward short dramas. In addition, the development of online self-made skits cannot be separated from the macro context of economic development.

In the context of rapid economic growth in China, iQIYI, Youku and Tencent Video, as the important producers of online self-made content, rely on the resource advantages of Baidu, Alibaba and Tencent, which not only protect the capital market of online self-made dramas but also attract an influx of capital, thus promoting the production and industrial optimization of online self-made dramas. According to *China Online Video Market Annual Report 2021*, compared with the shrinking investment scale of the TV drama market, the attraction of the online drama market to capital is still on the rise (particularly from 2018 to 2020), and the expansion of investment scale provides an important foundation for the high-quality production of online self-made dramas (Analysis International 2021, 6). From the overall social context and technical factors, the development of the Internet has met the diversified and personalized needs of Internet users, and the continuous influx of foreign high-quality dramas has cultivated the aesthetic taste and expectations of local audiences to a certain extent. High-quality dramas all have light volume and high-quality production standards, and the trend of online self-made dramas toward high-quality and short dramas also conforms to the international trend.

Internet-made short dramas highlight video websites as the main producers and broadcasters. At present, the main body of online self-made dramas basically find themselves competing with iQIYI, Tencent Video and Youku, Mango TV, Bilibili and Sohu Video. The production of online self-made content has become an important means of differentiated competition among major video websites, which is of great significance to the construction of brand images. Since it was officially launched in 2010, iQIYI has been expanding its content creation and production based on the innovative concept of the platform. In 2017, *Burning Ice* refreshed the audience's cognition of domestic online dramas with production standards that are comparable to those of Quality Dramas. In 2018, Strange Suspense Theater was an attempt to attract specific audiences with genre dramas and form a long-term effect with multiple dramas. Mist Theater has been renovated on this basis, and many suspense-type dramas have been launched that meet the needs of different audiences, forming a layered and vertical audience.

More importantly, iQIYI has adopted an industrialization model to operate the theater: in the production of dramas, 12 episodes are used as the standard, and suspense as the main genre. The solo broadcast of the platform can attract more users to settle in; for example, *Kidnapping Game* (2020), first launched by Mist Theater, focuses on suspense and love. As the first online drama adapted from Keigo Higashino in China, it also plays a role in promoting Mist Theater. Likewise, *The Bad Kids* (2020) really makes Mist Theater deeply rooted in audience's hearts. After that, Mist Theater once stopped broadcasting, *Sisyphus* (2020) and *Crimson River* (2020), which returned after two months, continued the brand effect created by the previous two dramas, despite the fact that their overall evaluations were not high. Finally, *The Long Night* (2020) had the blessing of the main creative lineup and original works, also won a high evaluation by virtue of the innovation of multiple time and space narrative techniques. All of these reflect iQIYI's innovative decisions on content and communication.

The Genre Integration and Narrative Innovation of Mist Theater

The suspense drama can trigger the audience's stimulation points from the story model, structure and plot, and mobilize their inner emotions (He 2018, 37–39). This is in line with the current market potential of the "Stimulating Drama" setting, where the strong plot and fast narrative characteristics of the suspense theme itself are suitable for the narrative volume of short dramas. Take Netflix as an example: in its self-produced content map, from the earliest political suspense drama, *House of Cards* (2013), to *Stranger Things* (2016) and other crime and science-fiction suspense dramas, to the development of the international market, genre fusion has been its main method for attracting users.

Likewise, Mist Theater is also an integration of the suspense genre and the short-drama format. The genre classification of the Mist Theater shows that it contains multiple types of fusion, such as suspense and crime. At present, there is no clear definition of this kind of drama in China. However, these suspense short drama all take crime as the core, which has the characteristics of traditional police and bandit dramas. On the whole, this kind of drama constructs a narrative structure with clear distinctions between good and evil and binary opposition, which illustrates the redress of people's grievances, the praise of loyal officials, the affirmation of authority and the maintenance of the national system. Coupled with the invisible control of the mainstream ideology, the parts of evil being punished and justice being done are often enlarged (Hao 2008, 135), forming a relatively simple and solidified narrative mode.

These types of TV dramas exist in two processes of creation and appreciation: on the one hand, grasping and appreciating the overall formal structure; on the other hand, organizing and creating some specific artistic elements (Hao 2008, 135). Although, to a certain extent, it is still subject to the influence of traditional TV genres, Mist Theater takes suspense as the main element and adds sub-elements of romance, crime, family and science fiction, among others. The infiltration of other genre elements and subtle changes have had the effect of dissipating the serious realistic attitude and questioning spirit behind the genre of police dramas (Hao 2008, 289), breaking through the ideological constraints of creation to meet the needs of a diversified audience.

Genre fusion is an important creative technique for content production on video sites. Even in the United States, where film and television are highly genre driven, to avoid falling into homogenization, productions often borrow different genre elements from each other to accomplish genre fusion and multiple expressions. Take Netflix's *Stranger Things* (2016) as an example (Table 2.1): it is a science-fiction mystery set in Indiana in 1983 that pays homage to many classics by referencing or copying genre elements.

The same is reflected in several of Mist Theater's productions (as shown in Table 2.2). The genre-blending characteristics of Mist Theater can still be examined according to its basic narrative components: plot, scene and

Table 2.1 Creative approach to the genre fusion of *Stranger Things*.

Title	Year	Type	Reference Element	Presented in the Series
Stand by Me	1986	Children, adventure	Four kids	The adventure of four partners
Silent Hill	2006	Suspense, horror	Roles and details	Mothers who save children; otherworldly white drifts
E. T.	1982	Science fiction	Plots	Eleven being hidden; wearing a wig and pretending to be an identity
The Thing	1982	Science fiction, suspense	Title and image of the monster	The title of the play *Stranger Things*; similar monster appearances
Alien	1979	Science fiction, horror	Appearance	Similarity of monster images
The X-Files	1993	Suspense, thriller	Plots	Conspiracy of government experiments; super-powered children

Table 2.2 The genre fusion of Mist Theater.

Title	Type	Reference Genre Element	Presented in the Series
Kidnapping Game	Suspense, love	Evil women in film noir; Plot setting in films like *Better Days* (2019)	Female dominated; the main characters as each other's protector
The Bad Kids	Suspense, family	Juvenile crime and kid's adventure genre	The summer adventure of three children
Crimson River	Suspense, crime	Environmental elements in film noir; bad weather in the suspense genre	Rainy and foggy weather in the sense of suspense
Sisyphus	Suspense, science fiction	The same genre such as *Source Code* (2011)	Structural crossing techniques
The Long Night	Suspense, crime	Films like *The Life of David Gale* (2003)	Similar themes and plots

character (Schatz 2009, 28). Specifically, *Kidnapping Game* (2020) begins with the body of the kidnapped person, and launches two narrative clues around the two periods before and after the 10th day, with the kidnapping game of male and female protagonists as the main line. With the development of the plot, the leading role of the heroine in the whole event gradually emerges, reflecting the function of manipulating-deceiving or sometimes domesticating the hero (Schatz 2009, 121), which has the characteristic of film noir's character prototype. Likewise, *Crimson River* (2020) uses elements such as night, rain and fog to render emotions in the scene and atmosphere, and reflects film noir's usual technique in visual presentation. When this kind of drama involves a crime plot, it often sets off the atmosphere with the gray overall tone. Although *The Bad Kids* (2020) continues the dark style of suspense drama in terms of plot and music, the whole story takes place in a small coastal town in the South of China, and the hot sunshine in mid-summer contrasts with the shadow implied by the criminal event. On the whole, Mist Theater enriches the original genre layout by means of genre fusion and, on this basis, forms a diversified expression of genre narrative.

The family and daily characteristics of TV communication have established the dominant position of long dramas in the whole TV drama creation (Song & Yuan 2002, 41), and the time advantage determines TV series long narrative tradition to a certain extent. Traditional police and bandit dramas and early network suspense dramas often promote the continuous extension of the plot through continuity, modeled characters and narrative. The TV series *The VI Group of Fatal Case* (2001) illustrates the process of police cracking down on crimes and investigating cases through the unit story structure of one episode and two cases with staggered development. *Day and Night* (2017) is a self-made suspense drama produced by Youku, but the whole drama has a major case that runs through the main line, interspersed with six branch cases, and still has the characteristics of traditional police and bandit dramas in terms of its narrative. This linear narrative mode with the nested structure of "big case plus small case" is not limited by the duration, so it has much room for creativity. However, the larger number of episodes also causes the slow rhythm and redundant plot of long dramas. With the short-drama development of online self-made dramas, Mist Theater has made new breakthroughs in narrative structure, audiovisual language and theme expression on the basis of continuing traditional narrative types, reflecting the trend of the high-quality content of online self-made short dramas.

The traditional "unit drama" and "serial drama" mode, together with the lengthy linear narrative, make the narrative of this kind of drama series too limited. However, several short series from Mist Theater have renovated the traditional narrative mode in different forms. *Kidnapping Game* (2020) constructs two narrative times and spaces, taking crimes committed 10 days ago as the main narrative line and the solving of crimes 10 days later as the secondary narrative line. At the same time, it is mixed with multiple branch lines, and the main and secondary narrative lines are constantly cross-edited, which not only complements the narrative content but also creates more suspense for the drama series. *The Bad Kids* (2020) is developed in two worlds—those of adults and children—and narrated through two crime lines. The plot line of the police is included to pave the way for solving the case later on. Zhang Dongsheng and Zhu Chaoyang are not only the contrast between adults and children but also imply an inheritance relationship. Moreover, Yan Liang's and Pupu's character stories are included as the secondary lines, adding more narrative clues to the main line.

Crimson River (2020) consists of two cases committed around 20 years ago, which constitute two times and spaces of memory and reality, while *The Long Night* (2020) spans three times and spaces, and flashbacks offer clues about the subway corpse-dumping case taking place in the present, and so gradually reveals the truth of the past. *Sisyphus* (2020) has the characteristics of a traditional unit drama. The first four episodes form a model of one episode and one unit, and each unit is independent and complete. With the addition of sci-fi elements, the audience can follow the characters' perspectives into a specific space-time at the beginning of each episode, and return to reality at the end of the story because they cannot reverse the situation. This customs-clearance narrative mode creates the sense of playing games. In addition, the time and space of each episode are advanced on the basis of the previous one, but the hero, Zhang Haifeng, cannot get rid of Zhao Binbin's control of death or the ending in any situation. The title *Sisyphus* (2020) is undoubtedly a reference to this sense of fatalism.

TV art is built on the end of a stable quadrilateral, composed of time, space, vision and hearing (Dai 2004, 4). The volume of short plays has high requirements for narrative rhythm and narrative intensity. On one hand, the narrative rhythm is faster and the plot is more compact; on the other hand, the characters and actions alone cannot fully promote the plot, and the narrative function of audiovisual language can be brought into play, reflecting the creative characteristics of video art. Previously, police-bandit dramas focused on promoting linear narration with characters and dialogues. Spatial environment was often just a narrative background, and audiovisual language was relatively simple. In the choice of story space, Mist Theater not only fits the theme of the drama itself but also integrates the characteristics of geographical environment into its visual style, forming a unique spatial expression. *The Bad Kids* (2020) is set in Guangdong Zhanjiang, and the modernization process of the third-tier cities is relatively slow, which is similar to the context of the story in the 1990s. The southern coastal cities also conform to the scenes of aquatic products factories and barges in the play.

It is worth mentioning that many dramas from Mist Theater set the story background in Chongqing. Different from the traditional urban form, Chongqing has a very distinct staggered regional form in spatial expression because of its natural geographical environment, forming a diversified spatial expression of Mist Theater (Lu & Sun 2020, 29–33). First, *Crimson River* (2020) combines the rainy and foggy climate and terrain conditions of Chongqing, and the dark and humid environment increases the suspense of the narrative. The location along the Yangtze River is also in line with the plot setting that criminals use bamboo rafts to drift the victims' bodies down the river. Similarly, *Sisyphus* (2020) gave full play to the uniqueness of Chongqing's urban structure, and the magical three-dimensional structure and complex streets and lanes became the natural barrier for criminals, which made several chase scenes in the drama more thrilling. In addition, *The Long Night* (2020) uses Chongqing's multi-space to start a multi-line narrative, and the play constructs three times and spaces from 2000 to 2010: the 2000 plotline surrounds Hou Guiping's teaching in the mountains; in 2003, the timeline revolves around the investigation activities of Jiang Yang and others in Pingkang County; and in 2010, the story starts with the subway corpse-dumping case in an urban area. From mountainous areas to the county and towns to the city, the setting reflects the spatial layering of Chongqing, which is characterized by the coexistence of big cities and big rural areas, the interlacing of tradition and modernity, the contrast between mountains and water and the poverty and wealth (Yang 2013, 191–194). This drama uses a large number of transition shots to switch between times and spaces, which intersect and promote an orderly narrative, giving full play to the role of lens language. Mist Theater tries to break through the traditional technique of taking space as the background and conveys the theme of the work to the greatest extent in combination with the geographical characteristics, thus forming a representation of the genre's style.

The concept of family is one of the cores of Confucianism (Ma 1999, 22), and family culture is an important part of Chinese culture. Since the birth of Chinese TV dramas, there has been no lack of performance for families, and family ethics dramas have always occupied an important position in the territory of domestic TV dramas. From the perspective of Mist Theater, *The Bad Kids* (2020) directly points to the important influence of family education on teenagers' growth, and the three teenagers in the play finally commit a crime, which is not unrelated to the "aphasia" of their family education. In addition, several other dramas have considered the family at different levels. Yu Hai, the hero of *Kidnapping Game* (2020), was influenced by his family since childhood, and his online games reflect his psychological trauma.

In *The Long Night* (2020), the victimized female students in mountainous areas reflect the phenomenon of staying behind in rural areas and the lack of family education. The criminal in *Crimson River* (2020), whose actions originated from the experience of mistakenly thinking that his whole family died in a fire decades ago. The descriptions of family in these dramas reflect the discussion of one's family of origin in the present society to a certain extent. The criminals in traditional police and bandit dramas often are seen in facial makeup, and the descriptions of their criminal motives are relatively simple. From the Mist Theater, it can be seen that the characters begin a life of crime with profound family and social roots, and the scripts incorporate more realistic expressions and humanistic care, which further enriches their narrative depth and theme expression.

From this, it can be seen that Mist Theater, which is in line with the Quality Drama model, echo with HBO's quality TV to innovate the aesthetics and narrative structure of television (Jenner 2016, 257–273). In terms of genre creation, it is diversified to meet the audience's needs, and in terms of scripts, they combine narrative innovation with the trend of short dramas. In the cinematic sense of audiovisual language, regional spatial expression and localization of thematic expression, all reflect the development trend of homemade short dramas in China.

The Production Mechanism and Operation Mode of Mist Theater

The text cannot be viewed in isolation, but must be linked to the historical conditions of its production and consumption (Morley 2005, 69). The script form of online self-made skits was born on the Internet, and its high-quality content production trend was influenced by the social environment, media characteristics, industrial system and consumption patterns. Fine products used to be synonymous with high-quality products in the commercial field, and then gradually transferred to the field of cultural production (Hu 2004, 59). Cultural products of high quality, precise content and exquisite form are also called fine products. From the perspective of communication effects, high-quality online self-made dramas are often widely sought because of their high-quality scripts, and their market value can be continuously extended through industrial operations. On one hand, this continuity benefits from the practice of type production and pattern reproduction of texts recognized by the market; on the other hand, it comes from the subversion of the existing practice, that is, when the market capacity of a certain operation mode reaches saturation, the production subject needs to find new operation possibilities to attract users.

The success of Mist Theater is inseparable from its high-quality scripts. From the table below, it can be seen that the content sources of Mist Theater include Intellectual Property adaptation and original stories. These texts have passed the test of the market, have a certain audience base and quality assurance, and have the operability of film and television adaptation. The famous Japanese mystery writer Keigo Higashino's works have a certain popularity in China, and many have been successfully adapted to film and television. *Kidnapping Game* (2020) is adapted from one of his productions, but the popularity of this novel and its corresponding film and television dramas is not high. In the local adaptation, the interference of other films and television works can be reduced, so there is a relatively broad creative space. As a local speculative fiction writer, Zi Jinchen's *King of Reasoning* series, including *The Bad Kids*, *The Untouched Crime*, and *The Long Night*, has a certain popularity in the market. These works not only have advantages in plot and logic but also reflect reality and humanity, and have a certain fan base.

In 2018, under the short-drama effect of *Burning Ice* (2018), iQIYI launched Strange Suspense Theater, including many self-made suspense dramas, such as *Original Sin* (2018), *The City of Chaos* (2018) and *Last One Standing* (2019), and can be regarded as the predecessor of Mist Theater. The difference is that the former mainly regard theater as a collection of genre dramas, attracting the attention of genre users, but it does not form the scale and strategic operation of the latter.

Mist Theater has formed an industrialized operation mode from the aspects of production, dissemination and distribution. From the perspective of production, since 2014, video websites, as the main producers of online self-made dramas, have promoted the transformation of the content production mode. According to the main producers, online self-made dramas can be divided into three modes: video websites plus content producers, video websites plus advertisers and video websites' complete independent production (Cao 2011, 116). iQIYI takes the first as the main form of content creation in the Mist Theater, in which video websites participate as producers and investors, while content production is undertaken by professional film and television companies, and mature content producers guarantee the quality of content production (Table 2.3). Since its establishment in 2015, Wuyuan Culture has produced many self-made suspense dramas with high reputations, including *Day and Night* (2017) and *Unforgiven* (2016). Dramas such as *Burning Ice* (2017) and *Original Sin* (2018), previously produced by Wannian Film Industry, are representative works of iQIYI's self-made suspense dramas, which have accumulated team resources and production experience for the creation of Mist Theater.

As far as communication strategy is concerned, on one hand, taking 12 episodes as the production standard of five dramas conforms to the inherent "ritual sense" of genre dramas, which not only ensures the overall tonality of the works but also constructs the brand image of Mist Theater. On the other hand, Mist Theater has gradually gained market recognition and brought more commercial value to iQIYI through the effective integration of drama broadcast sequence and broadcast cycle. Judging from the broadcasting sequence of the five dramas, the love element of *Kidnapping Game* (2020) has wide acceptance, which opens up the audience market of Mist Theater. *The Bad Kids* (2020), which follows closely, has aroused constant heat

Table 2.3 Content production subjects of iQIYI Mist Theater.

Name of Drama	Co-producers	Production Company	Content Source
Kidnapping Game	iQIYI, Wuyuan Culture	Wuyuan Culture	Keigo Higashino's *Kidnapping Game*
The Bad Kids	iQIYI	Wannian Pictures	Zi Jinchen's novel *The Bad Kids*
Crimson River	iQIYI, Wuyuan Culture	Wuyuan Culture	Original story
Sisyphus	iQIYI, Wuyuan Culture	Wuyuan Culture	Zhen Fuqun's original story
The Long Night	iQIYI	Haoji Pictures	Zi Jinchen's *The Long Night*

and concern with its excellent narrative ability and characterization; many details, such as scripted lines, soundtrack and opening and closing of the play, have also become a topic of constant discussion by the audience, and the dissemination and influence of the drama series have been expanding. It can be said that *The Bad Kids* (2020) has established the brand image of Mist Theater and realized the audience market's double recognition of drama series and theater.

According to the arrangement of the first two dramas, six episodes are broadcast every week and one episode every two weeks. Members can watch the dramas in time with their update frequency, while non-members need to wait for another week. *The Bad Kids* (2020) has introduced the option of "Advance on Demand"; after broadcasting two episodes, paid viewers can pay another extra to watch the broadcast episodes before the update on Member Day. This strategy fits the narrative characteristics of the episodes; specifically, *The Bad Kids* (2020) divides the narrative rhythm according to the drama points, leaving a certain suspense at the end of each episode and arousing the curiosity of the audience as to what will happen afterward, thus attracting users to pay to continue watching. In addition, although the Mist Theater stopped broadcasting for two months, *Sisyphus* (2020), which is inferior in terms of textual narration, still gets a certain degree of attention because of the market recognition accumulated by *The Bad Kids* (2020).

The Long Night (2020), although failing to reach the dissemination breadth of *The Bad Kids* (2020) due to the seriousness of the subject matter, also gained high market ratings. This drama adopts the same strategy as *The Bad Kids* (2020) in terms of broadcasting. iQIYI takes into consideration drama quality and the potential market in deciding the drama broadcast sequence and update frequency, and many excellent short dramas form a long-term effect. The suspense type attracts specific audiences, which causes psychological cluster effects for users, while theater functions as a "network virtual community" to continuously aggregate audiences. Through the approach of Attraction-Establishment-Continuity-Consolidation, Mist Theater has gradually built up its brand image.

High-quality self-made content is the embodiment of the platform's differentiated competitiveness, and the creation of short dramas and practice of theatricalization further enhance recognition of the platform. For the Mist Theater, its success cannot be separated from the accurate positioning of types and themes and the effective planning of production and dissemination. Type development and content production are carried out according to users' needs, and users are continuously accumulated through the typed theater mode and high-quality homemade content, attracting users to pay for high-quality content, thus bringing more market value to the platform to feed back into content production and forming a virtuous circle of industrial operation.

The high-quality production and operation of iQIYI's Mist Theater has certain enlightening significance for the content production of domestic online homemade short dramas. Additionally, it should be noted that the strategic broadcasting of Mist Theater reflects the uneven quality of dramas created by the theater, and the reputations of *The Bad Kids* (2020) and *The Long Night* (2020) are much better than those of other films. Although *Sisyphus* (2020) and *Crimson River* (2020) have the advantages of a creative team and production ability, they fail to innovate on the basis of ensuring the quality of the scripts. They are only a shell with suspense, with no foundation for the story.

Because the revenue source of domestic video streaming platforms has always been primarily advertising and member income, inserting advertisements in dramas has become a feature of domestic dramas, and short dramas cannot achieve relatively long-term benefits as long dramas can. Although the theater model has made up for this deficiency to a certain extent, there are still many blunt advertisements in several dramas of Mist Theater, which not only hinders the fluency of the overall narrative but also destroys the audience's immersion in the viewing process. In addition, due to the lack of copyright protections in China, pirated videos can be found on the Internet shortly after the platform is updated, which hinders the accumulation of user stickiness on video websites.

In the final analysis, the refinement of domestic online self-made short dramas should be based on text narration and should seek narrative breakthroughs within the limited narrative capacity of short dramas. However, the revenue model of video websites still has a lot of room for development. If the problems of advertising and copyright cannot be improved in the short term, it is important to explore other revenue paths besides advertising and memberships for the long-term development of the platform.

Concluding Remarks

The research and analysis of Chinese film and television culture will not get a correct understanding if we simply examine the artistic texts without examining the external institutional environment and restrictive forces at the same time (Hao 2008, 73). Under the unique cultural context of the country, the film and television creation of crime themes has always been subject to system management and review. As early as 2004, the country issued relevant policies to control the content and scale of the subject matter involved. After that, this theme gradually developed with the relatively broad influence of the Internet, which promoted the rise of online homemade suspense dramas. However, under the restrictions of the synchronization of network censorship and dominant culture, the development of network suspense types is facing many restrictions and difficulties. Furthermore, with the rise of streaming media represented by Netflix, the market demand of online self-made content has been expanded again under the influence of the COVID-19 pandemic. Foreign self-made dramas with streaming media have influence in mainland China and have shaped the aesthetic expectations of local audiences. Netflix has not yet entered the Chinese market, and there is still a large market space for domestic video websites to develop.

Clearly, the production of short dramas reflects current development trends at home and abroad. Mist Theater explores more types of expressions, narrative breakthroughs, cultural characteristics within the established framework, and innovates the production mechanism and operation mode in combination with the local context, which provides an important reference for the high-quality production of local online self-made short dramas.

References

Analysis International. 2021. *China Online Video Market Annual Report 2021*, p. 6.

Cao, S. S. 2011. "The Concept and Practice of "Self-Produced Drama on the Internet"", *Modern Communication (Journal of Communication University of China)*, vol. 10, pp. 113–116.

Capital Film and Television Development Think Tank. 2018. *2018 China TV Series Industry Development Report*, p. 5.

Dai J. H. 2004. *Film Criticism*. Beijing: Peking University Press, p. 4.

Ding, Y. 2014. "UGC+PGC: Exploring the Production Mode of Online Self-Produced Dramas", *Audiovisual World*, vol. 4, pp. 69–73.

ENdata. 2015–2016. *China Web Self-Produced Drama Market White Paper*, p. 6.

Feng Z. Z. 2016. *Research on the Creation Method and Dissemination Mechanism of Web Drama*. Beijing: China Federation of Literary Press, p. 33.

Hao. J. 2008. *Chinese TV Dramas: Cultural Studies and Genre Studies*. Beijing: China Film Press, pp. 73 & 135.

He, J.Z. 2018. ""Stimulating Drama" Is Underway", *China Radio and Television*, vol. 20, pp. 37–39.

Hu, Z. F. 2004. *Chinese Television Planning and Design*. Beijing: China Radio and Television Press, p. 59.

Jenner, M. 2016. "Is this TVIV? On Netflix, TVIII and Binge-Watching", *New Media & Society*, vol. 18, no. 2, pp. 257–273.

Liao, L. & Wu, B. 2009. "The Crux and the Way Out of Domestic TV Dramas Nowadays: Taking the Programming and Production Mode of American Dramas as an Example", *Communication Media*, vol. 2, pp. 44–47.

Lu, C. X. & Sun, L. 2020. "Spatial Practices and Cultural Representations of Urban Cinema in Chongqing in Recent Years", *Film Review*, vol. 3, pp. 29–33.

Ma, G. Q. 1999. *The Family and the Structure of Chinese Society*. Beijing: Cultural Heritage Press, p. 22.

Morley, D. 2005. *Television, Audience and Cultural Studies*, trans. Shi Anbin. Beijing: Xinhua Publishing House, p. 69.
Osur, L. 2016. *Netflix and the Development of the Internet Television Network*. Syracuse, NY: Syracuse University Press, p. 83.
Schatz, T. 2009. *Hollywood Genres: Formulas, Filmmaking, and the Studio System*. Shanghai: Shanghai People's Publishing House, p. 28.
Song, J. L. & Yuan, X. W. 2002. *The Art of Television Drama Scriptwriting*. Beijing: China Radio and Television Press, p. 41.
Ttacc.net. 2016. last modified Octorber 20, 2014, http://www.ttacc.net/a/news/2014/1020/31784.html
Yang, H. B. 2020. "The Development of Web Short Drama Chart and Content Construction", *Contemporary Television*, vol. 8, pp. 91–94.
Yang, H. T. 2016. "Key Words of Chinese Web-Based Self-Produced Dramas", *Contemporary Television*, vol. 6, pp. 37–39.
Yang, S. H. 2013. "Experimental Presentation of "Heterotopia" in the Contemporary Chongqing "Film City"", *Contemporary Cinema*, vol. 1, pp. 191–194.
Wu, Q. Y. & Du, H. 2015. "The Year of Game and Divergence: An Overview of the Development of China's Self-Produced Online Drama in 2014", *Contemporary Film*, vol. 3, pp. 188–192.
Zhou, C. Y. 2016. *A Post-Modernization Study of Domestic Web-Based Self-Produced Short Dramas*. Nanchang, China: Nanchang University, p. 8.

Chapter 3

WHAT ARE THEY BULLET-SCREENING ABOUT? A CONTENT ANALYSIS OF BULLET SCREEN COMMENTS ABOUT *CRIME CRACKDOWN* (2021)[1]

Xiaying Xu and Qingyuan Zhao

One of the key differences between Chinese video-streaming platforms (VSPs) and Netflix is the bullet screen option. Bullet screen, or *"Danmaku"* in Japanese, and *dan'mu* in Chinese, refers to the overlaid audience comments flying from right to left across the screen. These comments are displayed in the timeline when they were created, so later viewers may see exactly what comments have been left at a certain point in time during the show. Thus, the bullet screen is synchronous for the viewer, and also a form of asynchronous and trans-spatial interaction between the comment creators and their readers.

There have been many studies on the bullet screen. Its origins in the Japanese video website Niconico.jp in 2006 and how it became popular in China have been thoroughly described (Liu et al. 2016; Ni 2017). Chinese VSPs such as LeTV, iQIYI, Tencent and Sohu adopted the bullet screen feature in 2014. Youku and Tudou adopted it in 2015. It has since become a default feature of Chinese VSPs.

We analyzed 24,937 bullet screen comments from *Crime Crackdown* (2021) on Tencent Video, with the assistance of the data-mining software Pycharm. The 28-episode drama series *Crime Crackdown* (2021) was produced by Shanghai Tencent Penguin Film Culture Communication Co., Ltd, a subsidiary of Tencent, the leading listed company in media and communication in China. The show premiered simultaneously on the Beijing TV Station

---

[1] This chapter is funded by the BNU–HKBU United International College Faculty of Humanities and Social Sciences Research Fund, project code A2037.

Dongfang TV and online on Tencent Video on August 9, 2021. It reached 5.5 billion views as of March 2022 and received a rating of 8.9 points (out of 10 on Tencent Video). This chapter focuses on why the bullet screen is such a widespread functionality in China, what audiences bullet-screen about and how the bullet screen affects the viewing experience of TV series online, especially in the case of suspense genres.

Understanding the Bullet Screen

Bullet screen culture was first popular among viewers described as "Otaku," a Japanese word for the group of people interested in consuming anime and manga online who live in their "two-dimensional" world. This shared subcultural interest can be associated with bullet screen in-group comments. The bullet screen thus offers a sense of "social presence," according to Ni (2017). The concept of "social presence" was first raised by Short, Williams and Christie. They defined social presence as "the degree of salience of the other person in the interaction" (Short et al. 1976, 65). Most of the VSPs allow viewers to adjust the transparency of the bullet screen, or to turn it off entirely. Ni found that both non-transparent and semi-transparent bullet screen comments generate a sense of joint-watching (Ni 2017, 38). As Liang Xu (2018) describes, this joint-watching experience can be conceptualized as a virtual living room, where viewers seem to be watching the show at the same time and communicating with others synchronously, emulating a traditional living-room setting. This makes viewing online a less lonely activity, especially when in a collectivist culture like that of China.

The comments are "carnivalesque" and require a certain "entry threshold" and "an agreed-upon language system" in reaction to specific plots and visual elements, as Chen et al. (2013) observed in their ethnographic study of Bilibili.com, the most representative and earliest website to implement the bullet screen in China. Put simply, bullet screen posters comment from an insider perspective, and their posts may be embodied with rich intertextual allusions. In her doctoral dissertation, Xianwei Wu (2020) analyzed the intertextuality of bullet screen comments on Bilibili.com in detail. While agreeing with Harold and Marolt's (2011) comparison of Chinese online culture to that of the Bakhtinian carnival, Wu observed the heavy use of references in bullet screen comments. "Reference[s] can include anything from anime culture, *bilibili* culture, popular culture, internet culture or even historical references" (Wu 2020, 91). Thus, this heavy use of references shapes the "entry threshold" for "ordinary" viewers, as it requires insider knowledge. Identifying these references forms a collective community. Writing this type of comment is also a way to reach out to other viewers who have similar experiences, as a way of expressing mutual acknowledgment (Wu 2020, 99). Wan Anan, Leigh Moscowitz and Liwan Wu further suggest that users may feel a sense of belonging and gain more psychological well-being from bullet screens (Wan et al. 2019, 212). The bullet screen is certainly a form of convergence culture described by Henry Jenkins (2006), representing the growing importance of the role of audiences in the co-creation of media content. At least in China, the three leading VSPs feature bullet screens, and Bilibili, the Chinese version of YouTube, became popular for its bullet screen culture.

Intuitively, bullet screens may seem distracting, as they require multitasking: watching the original content, viewing others' bullet screen comments and writing or responding with further comments. However, many studies have shown some positive sides of this activity. For example, Wan et al. (2019) found that users who participated in this activity found it enjoyable. Other studies suggest that bullet screening makes online watching more engaging (Liu, Suh & Wagner 2016). It has also been associated with the individual preference for multitasking (see Ni 2017).

We may ponder what viewers bullet-screen about. Chen et al. (2013, 19–24) proposed a categorization of bullet screen comments into three categories: comments based on the content of the video; comments irrelevant to the words in the video, such as random chats between posters; and comments in the form of symbols, icons or emoji. Xu (2018) categorized bullet screen comments into four groups: comments about their motivation to watch the show; comments about the images or sound and spoken content; comments about the acting; comments interpreting the show; and comments in reaction to previous comments. This reminds us of what Liebes and Katz termed "critical decodings" and "referential decodings" in television viewing in their classical study of *Dallas* (Liebes & Katz 1990). Critical decodings refer to evaluative assessments, such as whether the acting is good, or if the production value is high. Referential decodings have to do with relating the image to reality. These assessments may serve as mutual aids for legitimization, orientation and interpretation in television watching (Liebes and Katz 2016, 280–300). It is possible that this mutual aid may be made more immediate with the bullet screen.

The review above provided a theoretical sense of what bullet screens are. However, not many studies have investigated what Chinese audiences are talking about while watching television online, especially when a suspense genre is on show. A question arises on whether bullet screen comments would spoil the show (spoiler comments) and whether these patterns of bullet screening can be found in a long-running TV series. We may also ponder how bullet screening affects the viewing experience in crime and suspense genres. (See Chapter 2 for the rising popularity of the Mist Theater and suspense genre online in China).

The Popularity of *Crime Crackdown* (2021) in the Context of Mist Theater

The success of the show *Crime Crackdown* (2021) can be attributed to several factors. First, it is based on real and influential crime cases in China, screened and offered by the Chinese Central Committee of Politics and Law. As Wang and Lobato pointed out, the relationship between the state and the platform in China is not the same as that in the West. The Chinese government is concerned about cultural content production, and one of the ways of keeping control of the cultural market is to offer what Anthony Fung has labeled as "soft nationalism through pleasure" (Fung 2009, 186) by means of state–platform collaboration (Wang & Lobato 2009).

Second, it is a crime and suspense show featuring government officials and the police, a genre with successful predecessors. For example, *In the Name of People* (2017) radically broke the stereotypical representations of government officials and generated a lot of suspense about power relationships. *Burning Ice* (2017) is a crime and suspense drama, coproduced by iQIYI and Beijing Thriving Pictures, about a serial murder case. *The Thunder* (2018), an original iQIYI production, reproduced the cracking down of the biggest methamphetamine production case that took place in a small village in Guangdong Province, China. iQIYI Mist Theater series such as *Day and Night* (2017) and *The Bad Kids* (2020) further lifted market expectations for the crime and suspense genres, owing to their production value. Netflix purchased the international distribution right of *Day and Night* (2017) in 2017, indicating its competitiveness.

The cast of *Crime Crackdown* (2021) also deserves a few remarks. Its starring actors include Sun Honglei, Liu Yijun and Zhang Yixing. The former two are national acting award winners with a repertoire of works in suspense dramas, and Zhang is a handsome singer with relatively less acting experience. Famous actresses in this show include Liu Tao, who has won a number of national acting awards, and Jiang Shuying, an established actress with multiple representative works who has received several nominations for best supporting actress. The cast attracts a very large audience base that would produce a huge number of bullet screen comments on the platform.

Understanding bullet screen comments on *Crime Crackdown* (2021)

With data-mining technology, it is possible to analyze and locate bullet screen comments from VSPs, only requiring some algorithms codes and a few minutes. This allows us to conduct a large-scale content analysis on these comments, rather than basing our research on observations and qualitative textual analysis alone.

To understand what viewers are bullet screening in relation to *Crime Crackdown* (2021), with the assistance of the Python software PyCharm, we captured bullet screen comments from the VSP Tencent Video, from 7 out of the 28 episodes of the show (episodes 1, 2, 8, 14, 20, 27, 28), as shown in the figure below.

The capturing date started on September 15, 2021 and finished on September 17, 2021. A total of 124,547 comments were retrieved. On average, each episode of the show has 17,792 comments. We randomly sampled 20 percent of the comments from the seven episodes in chronological order for analysis, as shown in the following table:

Based on previous studies (Chen et al. 2013; Xu 2018) about the bullet screen and categorizations of audience talks about TV series and our own observations, we divided the samples into seven categories: (1) Fandom, (2) Intertextual comments, (3) Comments irrelevant to the plot of the show, (4) Critical comments, (5) Referential comments, (6) Affective comments, (7) Irrelevant comments.

Category 1: Fandom comments clearly target the actors and actresses, expressing a motivation to watch the show just because of that actor or actress, or are appreciations of specific actors and actresses. Examples of this category include: "Liu Yijun is very handsome!", "Sun Honglei I am here to see you!" "I love Jiang Shuying."

Category 2: Intertextual comments are those with references, allusions and insider knowledge. Without intertextual knowledge, some comments would seem nonsense, such as "Can you assure me of the sweetness of the melon?", which was a representative line from the actor Sun Honglei in the drama series *Conquer* (2003).

Category 3: Comments irrelevant to the plot of the show refer to synchronous or asynchronous interactions among viewers, such as their greetings, ritualistic utterances, statements of attendance, and so on.

Figure 3.1 Episodes from which we sampled bullet screen comments.

Table 3.1 Number of comments retrieved per TV series episode after sampling.

Episode Number	1	2	8	14	20	27	28
Number of comments	3669	3602	3376	3398	3387	3593	3912

Category 4: Critical comments refer to evaluations of the acting and discussions about the plots and production value of the show.
Category 5: Referential comments are those linking the show with reality, such as those connecting the show with real murder cases.
Category 6: Affective comments are emotional expressions based on the show, such as "Salute to the heroes," "May the country be prosperous and bring [*sic*] peace the world."
Category 7: Irrelevant comments, such as "Jenny I love you," which is an irrelevant utterance.

Both authors of this chapter participated in the coding. Before coding, the raw data was organized with SPSS, and 2,470 comments (10 percent of the sampled comments) were randomly sampled for a reliability test. Based on the understanding of the categories, we started our coding manually. In the SPSS Krippendorff's Alpha reliability text, the algorithm scored 0.8818, which is higher than 0.8, suggesting acceptable reliability.

Patterns of bullet screening throughout Crime Crackdown (2021)

The percentages of the bullet screen comments of each category in the sampled episodes are shown in Table 3.2.

Category 1: Fandom

Bullet screen comments on fandom mainly appear in the first two episodes and in the last episode, which is predictable. Some of these comments indicated the motivation to watch, such as:

> Zhang Yixin, wo lai le.
> [Zhang Yixing, I am here.]

Most comments in this category express the viewer's liking of an actor or actress, such as:

WHAT ARE THEY BULLET-SCREENING ABOUT? 43

Table 3.2 Percentage of bullet screen comments in the sampled episodes.

Crime Crackdown (2021) Coding Sheet	Episode 1	Episode 2	Episode 8	Episode 14	Episode 20	Episode 27	Episode 28
1 = Fandom	7.9	2↓↓	0.8↓	0.4↓	0.9↑	0.6↓	2.4
2 = Intertextual comments	10.4	9.1↓	3.6↓↓	3.3↓	2.2↑	2.1↓	2.9
3 = Comments irrelevant to the plot	17.5	10.5↓	8.9↓	14.1↑	18.0↑	19.4↑	29.1
4 = Critical comments	47.7	71.6↑↑	80↑	80.2↑↑	77.1↓	72↓	51.4
5 = Referential comments	2.9	4.6↑	3.3↓	0.6↓↓	0.6→	4.8↑↑	1.6
6 = Affective comments	11.5	1.5↓↓↓	3↑	0.4↓	0.7↑	0.1	8.4
7 = Irrelevant comments	2	0.8↓	0.4↓	1.1↑	0.5↓	1.1↑	4.1

Sun Honglei wo ai ni.
[Sun Honglei I love you.]

Jiang Shuying tai piaoliang le.
[Jiang Shuying is so beautiful.]

Zhang Yixing de shengyin tai hao ting le.
[The sound of Zhang Yixing is so lovely.]

In the first two episodes, comments of this category tend to be about expectations regarding the actors and actresses, for example:

Liu Yijun zhongyu yan hao ren le zhe ci.
[Finally, Liu Yijun is performing the role of a good person this time.]

Yixing shenme shihou chuxian?
[When will Yixing show up?]

In the last episode, more compliments about the actors and actresses appear, such as:

Zhang Yixing yan de zhen hao.
[Zhang Yixing acted so well.]

Zhang Yixing zai da xi zhong tai shuang le.
[Zhang Yixing is so handsome in the action scenes.]

Overall, bullet screen comments on fandom account for a very small part of all comments and drop significantly as the plot develops, meaning that audiences are drawn to other aspects of the show.

Category 2: Intertextual comments

Intertextual comments appear most frequently in the beginning and decline steadily afterward. In the first episode, such comments account for 10.4 percent and drop significantly in episode 8 to 3.6 percent. The bottom value is 2.1 percent, which is over five times lower than the peak value. This indicates that intertextual comments may generate a sense of insider community, but when the insider atmosphere is set up, intertextual references start to lose the function of screening and looking for peers.

Taking a closer look at the intertextual comments, a rich matrix of references can be drawn. One of the most frequently referenced bodies of texts is from "Liu Huaqiang," a character acted by Sun Honglei in *Conquer* (2003):

> Zhe gua bao shou ma?
> [Can you guarantee the sweetness of the melon?]

This comment appeared 110 times. It became a signature line of Liu, head of a gangster group, because he is challenging and protesting some cheating acts of the watermelon vendor, such as faking the weight of the melon, something so commonly experienced in our daily lives. This line signifies a form of unofficial justice, celebrated in the online society of China. This is also one of the "carnivalistic" occasions of bullet screening.

Other than referencing other lines, the most common form of reference is to refer to other characters in other drama series. The name Li Fengtian is referenced 32 times, as Li Fengtian is an impressive cold-blooded serial murderer in *Burning Ice* (2017). Below is a table of references.

These references shape the larger context of the show, providing a scope of collective viewing experience for the audiences. The joint-viewing experience is not only represented by the "presence" of others but also consolidated by the evidence of a shared viewing experience, manifested by the intertextual references.

Category 3: Interactions irrelevant to the plot

This category refers to (a)synchronous greetings, statements of membership or statements of presence that are not related to the content of the show. This category accounts for a steady proportion of all comments, and a lot of them can be understood as ritualistic. Toward the beginning of each episode, there were a lot of comments claiming to be the first to comment. A total of 293 "di yi" (Number one) was found in our data. This is understandable, as those sending this message were simultaneously sending it immediately when each episode went online.

The second most frequent comment in this category is "lai le" (here I am), which is a statement of presence and expresses a sense of joining and belonging. "lai le" appeared 263 times. The third most frequent comment is "san yuan" (three yuan). This is the amount of money subscribers of the Tencent Video platform need to pay to sneak preview one more episode of the show ahead of other subscribers. This is one of the main different business models compared to Netflix, which was later heavily criticized and abolished. However, at the time of showing *Crime Crackdown* (2021), this system was still at work, gathering "three yuan" from many viewers. When viewers pay extra money for viewing, some feel the imperative to leave a trace of the money,

Table 3.3 Intertextual comments and their sources.

Body of Intertextual Bullet Screen Comments	Frequency	Source of Reference	Explanation
Liu Huaqian; watermelon; Can you guarantee the sweetness of the watermelon?	213	*Conquer* (2003). TV series. Genre: Crime, suspense	Liu Huaqiang is acted by Sun Honglei, who acts in the role of the protagonist Li Chengyang in *Crime Crackdown* (2021).
Ma Dadan; Lao San	73	*Candle in the Tomb: The Lost Caverns* (2020) TV series. Genre: Horror, suspense	Ma Dadan, alias Lao San, is acted by Zhang Jinan, who acts in the role of Xiang Tain in *Crime Crackdown* (2021).
Li Fengtian	68	*Burning Ice* (2017). TV series. Genre: crime, suspense	Li Fengtian is acted by Nin Li, who acts in the role of Ma Shuai, the CEO of the Xinshuai Group, in *Crime Crackdown* (2021).
Box	20	*Go Fighting* (2016). Reality TV Show	Sun Honglei and Zhang Yixing, both actors in *Crime Crackdown* (2021), took part in *Go Fighting* (2016), during which Sun Honglei robbed the box from Zhang Yixing through a trick.
Yu Qian	17	*Ming Dynasty* (2019). TV series. Genre: ancient costume	Yu Qian was acted by Su Ke, who acts in the role of Da Jiang, in *Crime Crackdown* (2021).
Shang Yang	17	*The Qin Empire* (2009). TV series. Genre: political costume	Shang Yang is acted by Wang Zhifei, who acts in the role of Gao Mingyuan in *Crime Crackdown* (2021).
Xin Lin; Love Department	16	*Love Department Season 2* (2011)	Xin Lin is acted by Jiang Ruijia, who acts in the role of Mai Jia in *Crime Crackdown* (2021).
Xia Yu; Xie Houye	16	*Nirvana in Fire* (2015)	Xie Yu is acted by Liu Yijun, who acts in the role of He Yong in *Crime Crackdown* (2021).

Poisonous Bee; Wang Tianfeng	11	*The Disguiser* (2015). Genre: Espionage, suspense TV drama	Poisonous Bee is an alias of Wang Tianfeng, acted by Liu Yijun, who acts in the role of He Yong in *Crime Crackdown* (2021).
Shen Shu (Uncle Shen)	8	*The Age of Awakening* (2021) Genre: History, revolution, mainstream TV drama	Shen Shu is acted by Zhang Haotian, who acts in the role of the policeman Suo Dong in *Crime Crackdown* (2021)
Xiang Yu	8	*The Myth* (2010) Genre: Time-travel mythic TV drama	Xiang Yu is acted by Tan Kai, who acts in the role of Dong Yao in *Crime Crackdown* (2021).
Sha Li Bin	8	*A Hero* (2014) Genre: Period, legendary TV drama	Sha Li Bin is acted by Su Ke, who acts in the role of Da Jiang in *Crime Crackdown* (2021).
Luo Xiang/Zhang San/	8	*Luo Xiang on Chinese Criminal Law* Genre: educational media content on Bilibili.com	Luo Xiang is a professor at the Chinese University of Political Sciences and Law, and his video on criminal law went viral on Bilibili.com. Zhang San is a fictional name he used as a criminal
Ah Weng; Dong Gong Ah Weng	5	*Goodbye, My Princess* (2019) Genre: Historical romance TV drama	Ah Weng is acted by Zheng Xiaoning, who acts as Wang Zheng in *Crime Crackdown* (2021).
Hu Suozhang	5	*You Are My Glory* (2021) Genre: Contemporary romance TV drama	Hu Suozhang is acted by Zheng Xiaoning, who acts Wang Zheng in *Crime Crackdown* (2021).
Liu Bowen	5	*Zhu Yuan Zhang* (2006) Genre: History, costume TV drama	Liu Bowen is acted by Zheng Xiaoning, who acts as Wang Zheng in *Crime Crackdown* (2021).
Cao Poyan	3	*The Longest Day In Chang'an* (2019) Genre: game adaptation, costume, suspense TV drama	Cao Poyan is acted by Wu Xiaoliang, who acts as the villain Sun Xing in *Crime Crackdown* (2021).

thus commenting "three yuan" on the bullet screen. As they paid again and again for another episode, lament-style bullet screen comments appeared, such as:

"san yuan you san yuan, san yuan he qi duo."
[Three yuan after three yuan, so many three yuan.]

"San yuan you san yuan, jin tian zhongyu keyi zhisun le."
[Yet another three yuan. Finally, today I can cut off the loss.]

"Dou hua qian le, shuohua xiaozhang dian"
[We've all spent money, let's talk more proudly.]

This kind of bullet screen content embodies complex feelings. First, it may show a sense of superiority, as their posters are more than VIPs on the platform: they can afford even more. Second, this comment serves as a record of their consumption, especially when it was their first time to pay extra money for a sneak preview. The sneak preview started from episode 14, meaning that starting from then, normal subscribers needed to pay 3 yuan for each episode viewed ahead of other subscribers. A total of 14 episodes could be consumed in the sneak preview mode, which is 42 yuan. With 42 yuan, one could almost subscribe to Tencent Video for three months (45 yuan is the fee for a quarterly subscription). This accounts for the lamenting style of comments. As viewers paid for the sneak previews, they made remarks about the money they lost. In contrast, they allow themselves to speak in a more arrogant way, as compensation for the money they spent. Chinese traditional culture highlights humbleness, as many other cultures do, but the bullet screening site can be a place to be arrogant. Social norms are temporarily suspended.

iQIYI, Tencent Video and Youku Video collectively cancelled the sneak preview system on October 4, 2021, as they admitted this system hindered the benefits of subscribers of the VSPs after they received complaints from the consumers and criticism from the Shanghai Consumer Right Protection Committee (Huang 2021).

Category 4: Critical comments on the show and development of the plot

This category consists of the bulk of bullet screen comments. This form of comment shows a clear normal distribution pattern, with episode 14, in the middle of the 28 episodes, bearing the highest number of these comments, which declines toward both ends. Viewers may be attracted by celebrities in the beginning and greet each other as they start watching the show, but as the plot develops, viewers were increasingly attracted by the plot. Toward

WHAT ARE THEY BULLET-SCREENING ABOUT? 49

the end, as the resolution becomes more transparent, viewer attention was diverted back to interactions among themselves and expressions of emotions.

These comments may address the acting of actors and actresses. In addition to comments in a general sense, there are many comments on the details of acting, such as

> "Zhe zuijiao chouchu leilei yan de hao jue."
> [The twitch of Leilei's mouth corner is impeccable acting.]

> "Sunxing zhe yanji, zhe yanshen fenming shi ge bei yiqi de xiaohai."
> [Look at the acting of Sun Xing. The look on his eyes really signifies an abandoned boy.]

This may serve as a magnifier of the image, directing viewer attention to some specific details of the show, thus intensifying the viewing experience.

There are also comments related to mutual orientation or "mutual aid in the decoding," as categorized by Liebes and Katz, referring to social interactions that "help define what happens on the screen by filling the gaps in the plot or by identifying characters in the thick foliage of the Ewing family tree" (2016, 282). However, a straightforward definition of relationships between characters and content of the plot is, for one thing, prohibited by the platform, as spoiler comments are not allowed. Furthermore, as bullet screen comments appear synchronously with the plot, even the viewers do not know for sure about the show at the point of bullet screening. Therefore, mutual orientation may also be "mutual disorientation." While watching a suspense drama and watching many speculative comments, the suspense effect may be multiplied, as there are many disrupting opinions.

This kind of comment may appear at the beginning of the show, as not much of the story has been revealed. We may see viewers speculating about the identity of Li Chengyang, the protagonist.

> "Li Chengyang: daodi wo shi haoren haishi huairen?"
> [Li Chengyang: am I good or bad?]

> "Wo buxiwang Li Chengyang shi haoren, buran jiu mei shenme ke kan."
> [I hope Li Chengyang is a bad guy, otherwise there is not much to watch.]

> "Sun Honglei is ge wodi."
> [Sun Honglei is an undercover.]

At least three different theories about Li Chengyang coexist, and it is up to the viewers to decide which one they agree with. Viewers can post guesses about the identity of the characters, but there can be no revelation about plot development. Spoiler comments, referring to revelations about the plot, are strictly prohibited, as a conventional rule of bullet-screening. However, one of the most frequently appearing bullet comments is:

"Qian fang gao neng."
[Immense energy ahead.]

This line connotes something huge or breathtaking is about to happen imminently. It appeared 37 times in our sample. This line does not reveal any substantial plots ahead, but gives a warning to the viewers, and builds up the tension of the plot. It may appear before a murder is committed, or before some horrible images appear, such as someone jumping off a building. In such cases, it may be considered that the bullet screen comments have become a generic part of the suspense genre, jointly exerting some degree of the "structuring effect" of a genre, in John Frow's terms—for Frow, genre "is a set of conventional and highly organized constrains on the production and interpretation of meaning [...] its structuring effects are productive of meaning" (2015, 10).

These embedded lines of warning are performing a particular structuring effect, so inescapable that they become an intrinsic part of the drama. However, these warnings may not always be echoed with plots that are worth the warned attention. Thus, they add to the uncertainty of the viewing experience, forming another layer of suspense, interacting with the original content.

Other critical comments include comments on production value, especially on the filmic quality of the image. Thirteen mentions of the filmic quality of the show were found in our sample. However, no specific mention was made about what made the show "filmic." From the first occurrence of this comment in episode 1, it corresponds with scenes where the police are chasing a group of gangsters on a wharf, with a variety of camera movements, especially fast ones. This may remind viewers of Hong Kong gangster films.

Category 5: "Referential" bullet screen comments

Referential bullet screen comments are those that relate the content of the show to real-life experiences or criminal cases. As the show is based on several real cases provided by the Chinese Central Committee of Politics and Law, this category of comments often discusses and guesses the relationship between the show and real criminal cases. The table below is a comparison of the cases in the show and real cases.

WHAT ARE THEY BULLET-SCREENING ABOUT? 51

Table 3.4 Comparison of crime crackdown cases and real cases.

Cases in Crime Crackdown (2021)	Real Cases
Murder and burial of Mai Zili Mai Zili was the inspector of a construction project in the Yihe New Village, which aimed at linking villages together. He stuck to his principle of quality insurance of the construction project, which may add to the cost of time and money. Dong Yao, chief of that administrative district murdered Mai Zili under the will of Gao Mingyuan, the head of Cheng Teng Capital, who later kept Mai Jia, the daughter of Mai Zili, as his concubine. Gao Mingyuan was later sentenced and executed to death, and his accomplices were brought under the law as well.	**Murder and burial of Deng Shiping** In 2001, Du Shaoping, a laid-off worker in Xinhuang county, Hu'nan Province, obtained a schoolyard construction project through illegal means. Deng Shiping, a representative of that school and inspector of that project, found faults with Du Shaoping. Du Shaoping later murdered Deng Shiping and buried him in the schoolyard. Huang Bingsong, headmaster of the school and Du Shaoping's uncle, covered the case up and interrupted the investigation of the case by means of bribery. In 2019, the national crime crackdown office reconsidered the case and demanded a reinvestigation. They found 19 government officials related to this case. Du Shaoping was sentenced and executed to death, while Huang Bingsong was sentenced to 15 years imprisonment.
Sun Xing's raping case: The original name of Sun Xing was Gao He. He is the son of Gao Mingyuan, the boss of Chang Teng Capital, and He Yun, chief of the Police Station of Zhong Jiang city, where the story of this show takes place. Sun Xing murdered someone years ago and changed his identity to Sun Xing. Relying on his relationships with his parents, he continues his evil practices. Xu Xiaoshan accidentally recorded Sun Xing revealing his evil past and was falsely imprisoned by Sun Xing. Xu Xiaoshan's sister, Xu Yingzi, came to rescue him, and was raped by Sun Xing and his followers. Sun Xing's mother covered him up constantly. In the end, Sun Xing was sentenced and executed to death and his mother, He Yun, was also brought under the law.	**Sun Xiaoguo's raping cases:** In 1994, Sun Xiaoguo, an armed police school student, raped two girls in Kunming, Yunnan province. He was sentenced to spend two years in jail but bailed out at large costs. During April to June 1997, Sun Xiaoguo raped many girls and was covered by his mother, who was a government official. In 1998, Sun Xiaoguo was sentenced to death, but was not executed and the death penalty was suspended. His penalty was later reduced again and again through his mother's *guanxi* (relationship) with some government officials. Finally, a total of 19 government officials were prosecuted and Sun Xiaoguo was sentenced and executed to death in 2020.

(Continued)

Table 3.4 (Continued)

Cases in Crime Crackdown (2021)	Real Cases
Gao Mingyuan's case: Gao Mingyuan, boss of Chang Teng Capital, runs underground casinos and private banks in ZhongJinag City, earning money to bribe government officials to act in favor of his real estate projects. Dong Yao, district chief, among the men that are most corrupted and manipulated by Gao Mingyuan. Gao Mingyuan is sentenced and executed to death, with all assets confiscated.	**Hunan Wen Honglie's case:** Wen Liehong built his fortune by selling fruits in Changsha, and he later ran underground casinos and set up a usury organization. In 2002, Wen Liehong lent money at usury to entrepreneurs in Changsha and opened casinos. To seek protection, Wen Leihong bribed the deputy chief of Changsha Police Station with 20 million yuan. His biggest protector was the deputy provincial chief of the public security bureau. Wen Liehong committed over 30 criminal offenses with 10 injuries and two deaths. He was finally sentenced and executed to death in June 2019, with all his assets confiscated.

Bullet screen comments mentioning "*caochang maishi an*" (burial case in school yard) occurred 28 times. These comments appeared in one of the two following manners: affirmative with confidence or tentative with curiosity and a question mark. Similarly, comments about Sun Xiaoguo's rape cases appeared 36 times. Other referential comments include specific bribery items such as expensive painting works or guessing about which "archetypal" city corresponds to the one in the show. Two peak timings for referential comments occurred in episode 2 and episode 27. As the plot unfolds, audiences started to identify these cases in episode 2, and when the show concludes, audiences are reminded again of the real cases.

Category 6: Affective comments

Affective comments are those that express an emotional reaction to the show,. A clear pattern of this category of comments can be seen in Table 2, as they appeared most frequently in the first and last episode. Emotions of excitement, anticipation and ecstasy can be felt from comments on the first episode. Of particular interest to us is the comment "hahahaha." This is one of the Bakhtinian carnivaleque laughter at work. Carnivalesque laughter, according to Bakhtin's introduction of the French writer Francois Rabelais (1493–1553) and his literary work and its relation to Medieval folk culture, was rich in complexity. It is a festive humor, universal and all-encompassing, manifesting a sense of duality: affirming and negating, rejoicing and mocking (Bakhtin 1984). "Hahahaha" may sometimes fill the whole page of the screen.

Another significant sub-theme in this category is the expressions of goodwill toward the end of the show. Examples include:

Yuan zuguo gengjia fanrong changsheng
[May the country be more prosperous.]

Zhijin sao hei chu e yingxiong
[Salute to heroes that crack down crimes.]

Shenghuo meihao
[May our lives be good.]

Yuan Tiankong, buzai huzhuo
[May the sky be blue, not dirty any more.]

Category 7: Irrelevant bullet-screen comments

Irrelevant bullet-screen comments have no relation to content of the show. Interactive comments are based on the show. This is the key difference. Irrelevant comments account for a very small percentage of all comments. They include comments such as:

Wang Jiayao wo ai ni
[Wang Jiayao I love you]

Li Anqi zai ma?
[Li Anqi, are you there?]

Liu Ziyuan wo cuo le
[Liu Ziyuan, I was wrong.]

These comments take the screen as a platform for interpersonal communication. They appeared most frequently in the first and last episodes. A clear sense of detachedness can be associated with these comments. Yet, this can be interpreted as another form of "carnivaleque" online culture, as these comments show a disregard for the rules and social media norms of commenting.

Conclusion

Although bullet screen comments may seem fragmented, random and out of nowhere: evoking the Chinese idiom "seven mouth eight tongues," as Wu (2020) summarized by close content analysis, we identified several bullet-screening communication patterns related to the development of the plot from the beginning till the end. Essentially, critical comments have a positive correlation with the intensity of the plot: As the plot develops, it draws more and more critical comments, and when the audiences have a more confident sense of what is going on, their attention will be diverted to other factors such as complementing their favorite celebrities, interacting with each other or expressing emotions. Audiences greet each other toward the beginning of the show and say goodbye to each other toward the end. Comments of intertextuality appear toward the beginning as well, as audiences are starting to draw a matrix of textual references to the show they are currently watching. This is certainly a form of "collective intelligence," as described by Henry Jenkins (2006, 1–4). Audiences also help each other with clarifying character relationships and deciphering what previously happened, displaying what Liebes and Katz categorized as "mutual aid in the decoding" (2016, 281–285). No spoiler comments are allowed, but comments of warning abound.

Another central contribution of this chapter is the discussion of how bullet-screening, as "collective intelligence" and "mutual aid," affects the viewing experience of a suspense drama. Our argument is that these bullet screen comments, regulated by the rule of "no spoiler comments" set by the platform, add to the complexity of the genre and unpredictability of the suspense. Further studies may compare the degree of scaredness and nervousness while watching a suspense genre with or without bullet screen comments. A sense of the social presence of others may lower the degree of nervousness. However, as other research has suggested, bullet-screening enhances the level of engagement (Liu et al. 2016). As two contrary hypotheses coexist, this question is worth investigating.

VSPs in China have made the function of bullet-screening a default, and keep exploring the affordance of this function, such as allowing more rainbow-like comments, or allowing "likes" of other comments. These comments can be seen as carnivalesque, breaking the rules of communication when people meet face to face and allowing them to oppose traditional culture and act proudly. Moreover, these comments may serve as word-of-mouth advertising, drawing more audiences to the show and contributing to the commercial logic of the VSPs. How bullet screening serves as word-of-mouth advertising can also be further elaborated, and an analysis of bullet screen comments from other genres may also be conducted with the help of python.

References

Bakhtin, M. 1984. *Rabelais and His World*. Bloomington: Indiana University Press.

Chen, Y. et al. 2013. "Toushi Danmu Wangzhan yu Danmu Zu: Yige Qingnian Yawenhua de Shijiao (Danmaku Websites and Danmuku Users: A Youth Subculture Perspective)". *Youth Exploration*. No. 6, pp. 19–24. DOI:10.13583/j.cnki.issn1004-3780.2013.06.006

Fung, A. 2009. "Globalizing Televised Culture: The Case of China". In Graeme Turner and Jinna Tay (eds), *Television Studies After TV*. New York: Routledge.

Herold, D.K., & Marolt, P. (Eds.). (2011). *Online Society in China: Creating, Celebrating, and Instrumentalising the Online Carnival* (1st ed.). London: Routledge.

Huang, Z. 2021. "iQiyi, Tengxun shiping, youku xuanbu quxiao chaoqian dianbo (iQiyi, Tencent Video and Youku Announced Cancellation of Sneak Preview)". *Xiao Xang Morning Post*. Retrieved from https://baijiahao.baidu.com/s?id=1712789937250764800&wfr=spider&for=pc

Jenkins, H. 2006. *Convergence Culture: Where Old and New Media Collide*. New York: New York University Press.

Liebes, T. & Katz, E. 1990. *The Export of Meaning: Cross-Cultural Readings of "Dallas"*. Oxford: Oxford University Press.

Liebes, T. & Katz, E. 2016. "Mutual Aid in the Decoding of Dallas". *The Communication Review*. Vol. 19, No. 4, pp. 280–300. DOI:10.1080/10714421.2013.1251789

Liu, L. et al. 2016. "Watching Online Videos Interactively: The Impact of Media Capabilities in Chinese Danmaku Video Sites". *Chinese Journal of Communication*, Vol. 9, No. 3, pp. 283–303.

Ni, Y. 2017. "A Study of Danmaku Video on Attention Allocation, Social Presence, Transportation to Narrative, Cognitive Workload and Enjoyment." Master thesis. Master of Arts in Media Studies. Syracuse University.

Short, J. et al. 1976. *The Social Psychology of Telecommunications*. London: John Wiley & Sons, Ltd.

Wan, A. et al. 2019. "Online Social Viewing: Cross-Cultural Adoption and Uses of Bullet-Screen Videos. *Journal of International and Intercultural Communication*. Vol. 13, No. 3, pp. 1–19. DOI:10.1080/17513057.2019.1610187

Wang, W. Y. & Lobato, R. 2009."Chinese Video Streaming Services in the Context of Global Platform Studies", *Chinese Journal of Communication*, Vol. 12, No. 3, 365–371.

Wu, X. 2020. ""Seven Mouths Eight Tongues": Interpretive Community and Ritual Practice in the Online Video Website Bilibili". Doctoral Thesis in Mass Communications. University of Iowa.

Xu. L. 2018. "Xuni Keting: Danmu Pinglun de Xinli Fenxi—Yi Dianshiju Renmin de Mingyi Weili (Virtual Living Room: A Psychological Analysis of Bullet Screening, with the Case of *In the Name of People*)". *Contemporary TV*. No. 7, pp. 81–82.

Frow, J. 2015. *Genre*. London: Routledge.

Chapter 4

CONTENT, PLATFORMS AND DISTRIBUTION: CHALLENGES AND PROSPECT IN THE FIELD OF WEBISODE PRODUCTIONS[1]

Wei Jiang and Pengcheng Zhou

Introduction

Online drama, or webisode, refers to series that take the Internet as the main communication channel and netizens as the main audiences. Compared with traditional TV drama, webisode is a novelty with its uniqueness and diversity, which is worth our study. As an emerging industry, China's online drama industry has developed considerably in recent years in terms of genre, quantity and quality, but at the same time, the industry is faced with the issues of simplification of theme selection, lagging of innovation ability and vulgarization of content production (Leng and Zhang 2015). Webisode creators' misreading of the characteristics of network drama creation and misunderstanding of the word "network sense" have led to the neglect of quality control and excessive adoptions of network IPs, and consequently have hindered the development of online drama creation and online drama industry (Zhao 2017). In addition, the rise of short video platforms has shifted the viewing habits of abundant netizens, and the traditional online dramas associated with long video platforms as the broadcasting channels have been challenged significantly, resulting in the emergence and prevalence of online vertical screen dramas (Cheng 2019). Meanwhile, due to the continuous requirements of the Party to cultivate a healthy and positive cyberculture (Xi 2016), the relevant authorities of the Chinese state have issued and updated regulatory

---

1 This research is financially supported by the UIC research grant II offered by the BNU–HKBU United International College (project code: R202046).

policies many times for this novel form of entertainment. And the policies are often seen by critics as a restriction on the freedom of online drama creation (Hu et al. 2020). Although researches have been conducted frequently on content and forms of online dramas and challenges faced by the online drama industry, a direct and deep communication with the practitioners from the industry is missing. As pointed out by Potter, formal interviews and dialogues with industry people can indeed bring a series of benefits to researchers (2018). Those benefits include access to unpublished expertise and a wider understanding of the operational thinking and belief systems that emerge from industry practices (Freeman 2016). This study filled the gap between the industry and academia, thus deepening our understanding of the online drama industry.

In any case, the Chinese government's policy on the online drama industry is bound to have an impact on the development of the industry. The consistency between relevant policies and public interests is considered to be mainly about whether the freedom of expression can be satisfied, whether the public's right to know can be guaranteed, whether online homemade series can play their educational functions and whether the rights and interests of teenagers can be protected (Li 2012). While the emergence of regulatory policies has not necessarily been welcomed by market participants seeking greater autonomy, the legislation and regulatory initiatives still represent a prominent role for the Chinese government in protecting the public interest (Shen 2012). The Chinese government has strengthened its supervision over the ideological tendency of webisodes (Wang 2017; Tian and Zhang 2017), cracked down on the problems of high remuneration for celebrities and disorderly market competition (Zhang 2017), and unified the censorship standards for online series and TV dramas (Tang 2019). The above policies related to webisode further sustain that the Chinese government regulates the Internet in a variety of ways, and there is systematic cooperation between local governments at all levels (Feng and Guo 2013). However, the fundamental contradiction of the current regulation of online films and series is that the censorship concept centered on series cannot adapt to the user-centered business idea of new media audiovisual content, and industry leaders should influence the formulation of policies to maintain the healthy development of the industry (Xu and Wang 2017). Moreover, Chan (2011) believes that provincial media, one of the disadvantaged media in China, have extremely limited space to participate in national policymaking, but they have considerable discretion in policy implementation. And in the webisode industry, the discretion that private webisode producers have on policy implementation is worth further discussion.

In recent years, the webisode industry has developed vigorously, and the webisode industry chain has begun to take shape. At present, the story creation of webisodes mostly comes from IP adaptation, and the webisode theme is based on the trend of mass segmentation and stratification (Li 2020). The production model of webisodes mainly relies on platform self-production, joint production between the platform and other companies and other company's main investment and control (Xiao et al. 2017). And the main profit channels of Chinese webisodes are account-sharing profit, advertising profit, fans profit, e-commerce profit, payment profit and copyright profit (Song 2020). From the perspective of industrial scale, affected by the epidemic, the overall consumption of webisodes shows a movement curve of sharply rising and then falling back to the average level, and the productivity of webisodes has not decreased but is steadily improving (Wang 2020). From the perspective of the spatial distribution of the industry, compared with the production network of traditional TV series, the enterprise location, core city nodes and strong connections between cities in the webisode production network are more concentrated, especially in the Beijing-Tianjin-Hebei region and the Yangtze River Delta (Wen et al. 2020). However, the dissenting voice is that the development of online drama in China and the linkage between television stations and the Internet can be found that webisode and TV drama are isomorphic (Zhan and Deng 2021). McQuail's view has guiding significance for the consuming end of the online series industry and the traditional TV series industry, that is, the audience differentiation under the influence of technological progress is an inevitable trend, but the extreme segmentation will not change the audience's similar demand for content out of the common mainstream values (Lv 2019). As can be seen from the above literature, the specific actions and strategies taken by practitioners of webisodes in the process of content development, production, distribution and profit-sharing have attracted a certain degree of attention in the academia, and the similarities and differences between webisode producers and traditional TV series producers in terms of the industrial chain are also being paid attention by scholars. This study further explored the above research hotspots so as to get a more suitable study results for the characteristics of industrial development.

This study focuses on a series of interviews with a group of influential webisode practitioners. Their biographies are as follows:

Xiaozhu WANG is an intimate collaborator of Jiang Wen, Feng Xiaogang, Zhao Baogang, Ye Jing and others, and has witnessed the process of the Chinese film and television industry moving step by step toward marketization for more than 20 years. In 2010, Wang joined Hairun Film Company, part of Hairun Film Group, China's largest production and award-winning production company, as script director. In 2011, he became the script director of Bona Film Group, the first Mainland Chinese film and television group listed on NASDAQ. In addition, he has been the producer, screenwriter, planner and actor of numerous film and television works, and has won the Golden Eagle Award for Best Production for the TV drama *Never Close My Eyes* and the Best Producer award for the TV drama *Farewell, Vancouver*.

Shuang QIN is Wang Xiaozhu's wife. She is also the scriptwriter of *Go Princess Go*, one of China's first online TV dramas to draw public attention. She has worked on *Let the Bullets Fly*, *Woman Gang* and *Special Identity* and other film and television productions.

Dandan YANG is a famous producer and executive supervisor. In 2008, she became the vice president and general manager of Beijing Orange Sky Golden Harvest Entertainment Co., Ltd., one of the influential Chinese film and entertainment groups. Her masterpieces include *Smell of Summer*, *Another Face* and *The Promise*.

Bangni BO is a well-known screenwriter and novelist. She has been involved in the screenwriting of *Prodigal Son Yan Qing*, *A New Dream of the Red Chamber*, *Mulan*, *Woman Who Flirt* and other film and TV works, and has written *Love You Like Bonnie*, *False*, *Fu Hua*, *Old Girl*, *See Good* and other best-selling books.

Jun YAO is a well-known webisode supervisor, producer. He served as the planning director of Youku and created Youku's original content team. He is now the founder and CEO of Beijing Hero Kiddo Media Technology Co., Ltd., a domestic head webisode company. He has planned, supervised and produced hot series such as *Old Boy*, *Never Expected* and *Women in Beijing*.

Q1: Could you briefly introduce the changes and development of webisode in recent years?

Bo: Sure. The first thing I noticed is that at the beginning many people looked down upon webisode because of its low entry barrier, poor production value, as well as marginalized topics. But it soon occupied a more important position, which could also be considered as the dividends of its rich subject matters.

Qin and Wang: I found it was easy for webisodes to become blockbusters with high click-through rate before 2015. Actors casted in these webisodes were not famous stars, and some of them were even newcomers. Although their production costs were low, they could still be well received because of the content, filming and acting skills. Since 2018, however, I realized that merely content or creativity was not enough. If there were no superstars, it was very difficult for webisodes to make achievements. High-quality drama series have gained popularity in recent years. They fully understand the audience's preferences and have a cast with famous actors who are good at acting. In terms of the content of TV series, almost all types of stories have been filmed. However, there are some novel themes of webisodes, for example, sweet and romantic dramas, which are very popular in recent years. They gain popularity as their theme meets the demands of the audience at a given time, rather than their creativity. On the other hand, there are some high-quality reality-themed dramas, such as *My Best Friend's Story* and *Nothing But Thirty*, which are well received and highly discussed by the audience. The era that low-budget webisodes can simply win with creativity has passed.

Q2: After the exposure of Fan Bingbing's tax evasion, National Radio and Television Administration (NRTA) launched new regulations in 2019, which stated that we should build up a standard about management, and set up an effective management mechanism. What did this affect the whole industry? Are there any difficulties or challenges for industry participants? And are there any new requirements for the content you created?

Bo: I believe lots of newcomers, who were at the bottom of this industry, did have a tough time. For companies, many projects became optional, so they could simply choose to terminate them, and this could give very hard time to those small writers. I remember back then I always saw friends complaining about their miserable life in Wechat Moments, and some of the small production companies even closed down their business. Even though, I still think for me it makes no difference. I mean I did panic a little as everybody said the situation was serious, but since writing scripts is a long-term project and we usually receive a bunch of money at one time instead of bit by bit, I haven't felt much changes. Just keep writing the scripts.

Qin and Wang: It is difficult to evade taxes now as the tax inspection is extremely strict. High remuneration is not allowed since contracts are required to be submitted to related administrations and get approvals from them. On the whole, the exposure of Fan Bingbing's "dual-contract scandal" has a positive impact on the film and television industry. The reduction of remuneration for actors enables producers to spend more budget on production itself. In the past, all the back images were shot with stand-ins. When the stars arrived, they just spent about 15 days to make up the shots of their front faces.

Yao: The income in the whole industry went down. Then, many shooting projects had to be shut down and I could have received some students to have internships in Beijing if not such a case.

Yang: From my point of view, it marks a turning point in the film and TV industry. Before 2018, people in our industry only focused on making money. They even never read the screenplay and only asked you who the director and actors were. Then they shot films and TV series, and released them in cinemas and TV stations. But after 2018, people got to know that it was necessary to do it now as the remuneration for actors had been regulated. Now, if you want to apply for a TV series or a movie, you have to report the contracts of the actors and creators and the entire budget, which means everything is in the open. Thus, it is difficult to evade taxes like before, and I think our industry develops in a good way. I don t know others' opinions, but for me, I won't evade taxes or sign dual contracts. And the focus of our industry has been shifted from making money to creating good film and TV productions.

Q3: In 2018, the National Radio and Television Administration announced that the remuneration for actors should not exceed 40 percent of the overall production cost. This new regulation seemed to bring our industry into a short period of recession in 2019. What difficulties did you face at that time? And how did you deal with them?

Yao: At that time, some actors' remuneration even reached to RMB 100 million, too expensive, and it seemed that the whole industry worked to pay for actors. So, from this point of view, the incident of dual contract was a good thing, but the real problem was the impact on the industry. Before 2018, though in competition, every online platform was making money. However, in 2018, limits were imposed on the number of webisode released on the platforms, for example, the market had required 100 projects before 2018, but it needed only 50 in 2018. Therefore, the supply–demand relationship was changed, and there was more supply than demand. Then, the interests of online platform decreased, so did the payment of producing groups. Regardless of the low interests, people had to work to earn their livings, so they continued their projects even with greater difficulties and lower revenues, as 100 projects needed to compete for 50 or even 30 chances. This was a bigger problem for an industry in B2B business model.
Qin and Wang: In 2019, we paid most of our attention to the development of IP. And there were two ways of creation: adaptation and original works. When making attempts to adapt books for webisodes, we found most of them couldn't be adapted successfully. That's why the project came to an untimely end before it had even begun. We finally realized that we should focus more on the creation of original scripts, rather than the adaptaion of novels. Not all subjects can be written for a script. In such a case, we select some original creative themes, such as the era drama and modern drama we are operating now, to create our own IPs.

Q3: The research in 2018 shows that themes of court competing tales, war, history, crimes, chivalry are prominent in the market, and this conclusion is generated from big-data platform so as people may tilt toward these types. Could you share about your considerations when choosing different themes?

Bo: We choose the theme based on our preference since conducting a project takes years to go. We don't want to spend a lot of time doing something we don't like.

Yao: We need to consider the target audience for sure. At present, the majority of webisode viewers are female, no matter in ratio, frequency or time. This situation has long existed, though one of the reasons may be there are scarcely any high-quality webisodes targeting male audience, you can see apart from this year and last year there are some projects of mysterious topic, most of the projects before last year are palace drama, real-life drama, romantic drama and other female-oriented drama. So, now we focus more on topics designed for female audience, and we classify these topics into two types. One of the types is real-life topic, and we produced this type of webisode before. In the future, we will still follow this trend, doing female-oriented projects.

Yang: I think it varies from person to person. For example, some producers want to make profits, some choose the theme based on their preference, while others focus on the potential of making good works. That is to say, producers have different ideas as well as the bosses of companies. There is not a fixed method to choose the theme. But in the past years, people do whatever they can to make profits, and now they make movies and TV series for the values promoted by the government.

Q4: What's your opinion about the impact of big data on the creation of webisode?

Qin and Wang: The market relies on big data to select the theme. The reason why many people ask me to produce romantic drama is that the data show it has a high click rate. Platforms are very clear that costume dramas are the most popular theme and they inform us of the situation. However, the data fails to cover all types of dramas. For example, there was no existing data about suspense, which made *Day and Night* difficult to be sold to the platform. After it was released, it received a high rating because of its content and high production value. Its good reputation motivated people to make suspense dramas.

Big data is sometimes good as it can help us find out the preferences of the audience. A romantic drama will always have sweet plots. But it is also exceptional, for example, the audience also likes the drama with both sweet and sad plots very much. The webisode itself is sweet, but you have to add some sad plots to it, so it becomes a sweet–sad drama. Eventually, the drama possibly expresses more sadness than sweetness. After watching the sweet drama for some time, a drama full of bitterness could be released and well received. Later, people will ask the question: Can we add bitter plots to the sweet–sour drama? In big-data-based approach, the chance of "letting a hundred flowers blossom" is relatively small. So now we cannot make webisodes completely according to the big data; otherwise, there will be no innovation.

Bo: It did have a huge impact on our team. I mean when you cooperate with the company, you will find that they are data-oriented and has a big saying about how to revise the scripts, while the role that producers can play is very, very small. The platforms and big production companies usually give their suggestions in a harsh and straightforward way. They have their own evaluation system which is strict and able to provide data like the degree of creativity, or the degree of online discussion. It really pissed me off when I saw the final graph that generated based on those assessment criteria, because it just didn't work in that way. The company insisted on revising the script until its score was above 8, or they wouldn't pay us money, so we just kept rewriting again and again, but still the score was below 8. Finally, the company suggested us to hire an optimization (revision) team, and we did. The score reached 8.5 after optimization, and I was full of joy, thinking that our script must be much better. However, I was totally wrong. All the optimization team did was to simplify, exaggerate the dialogues, making them superficial and ignoring the function of subtext. It was truly worse than before. But the company and evaluation system liked it. I still had lots of doubts about this system and the decision driven by big data. So I asked them to give me the highest-score script in this system, then I understood what it was all about: it avoided the worst script but also the best script, since the best one must have its own vibe and individuality. The first director we cooperated with told us the unique style of script is of most importance, and it is the only way to win. That was why he suggested us to keep it no matter what. Thus when I was cooperating with the data and the system, I was frustrated since it was impossible to communicate with them. Unlike producers, the suggestions given by the system was one-way, and I couldn't discuss with it. When we were shooting later, we found that the revised parts were bad as the actors could not read them smoothly. It was very straightforward. A good script helps the cast to act, and everything is fluent and smooth; while a bad script does the opposite. In fact, the so-called evaluation system is also made up of people who need to read four to five scripts a day. How can you say they are professionals? Even if you find 100 young audiences who tell they like the script or don't like the script, they cannot represent all the audience. That's why I hate the system. I made a lot of effort to save the script, but it would never be the same as the original. It was like a fully decorated house being smashed to pieces and built up again, so now it was impossible for me to do anything to make it look just like the beginning. The only thing I could do was to polish it as much as possible to make it fluent and complete.

Q5: In your opinion, how does the coronavirus pandemic affect the webisode industry?

Yao: I think it accelerates the process of testing the limits and potentials of this industry. But now the webisode industry has turned the corner I think, with a more vigorous market. In supply–demand chain, when the supply is higher than the demand, the interest for the industry will decrease, so what is needed is to cut down the supply, which is exactly what happens now since some companies were sifted out during the pandemic. In fact, this is a good thing.

Yang: Influenced by the pandemic, it is particularly difficult to get a working visa for a Korean director who is hired for the webisodes that we are going to make. And this has delayed our shooting time. For instance, the shooting time of our current project depends on when the Korean director can get the visa. We are now asking the Ministry of Foreign Affairs for help.

Q6: You started from making movie/TV series. Therefore, have you encountered any difficulties after transforming to make webisodes? Could you share your feelings or experiences in this transition with us?

Bo: In the past we usually worked with elder people that are experienced in this field, and to be honest, they are core groups who involved in the creation of some masterpieces. Even though sometimes they are resistant to accept new ideas, generally they have a deep understanding of drama. By contrast, now most of the people you work with, including the evaluation team and production team, are almost young generation. They are audience-oriented, producing whatever the audience like to see, and basically not familiar with drama. I feel like they pay too much attention to the favor of customers, like they always show us the favorites of the audience and say this is what we are going to make. This really upsets me. There are fewer and fewer people who really understand drama.

Qin and Wang: In the past, there were several big TV companies. The threshold for investment in movie and TV series was relatively low and the money was enough. As long as you can find a good director, you can start shooting. At that time, it took about RMB 20 million to find good directors, actors and scripts. In terms of releasing, there were 45 top TV stations and more than 20 satellite TV stations in China, and each satellite TV station was equipped with a local TV station. Because one drama can only be shown on two satellite TV channels, and the duration is limited—two episodes can be played a day, except for weekends and holidays.

However, with the rise of the Internet, advertising is put online, and it becomes easy for the online platforms to make money. An episode can even be sold to RMB 5 million on the platforms, but only RMB 3 million on the

TV station. Mainstream television companies can earn back the cost on the TV stations, and along with the sales online, one episode can make RMB 20 million profits at most. From the perspective of television companies, since the payment from TV stations can cover the production cost, the profit from online platforms is actually net profits. While from the perspective of TV stations, the advertising revenue is getting less, the price is getting lower, and the money is gradually given in a revenue cycle. With the online platform becoming rich and powerful, it is better for TV companies to directly invest into webisodes, since advertising is profitable, and the click rate of a single episode is also satisfying. So, investors will first go to the online platform, and only after making enough profits will they go to TV stations to search for extra interests. This eventually marginalizes TV stations. As a result, it has evolved into a situation in which the investors prioritize the online platforms over TV stations, so no matter how low the TV stations charge, they have less chances than the online platforms. With the marginalization of TV stations, gradually, the releasing and production of the dramas are all operated around the requirements of the online video platforms. The platforms first relied on contents that were not allowed on TV stations to attract people. The broadcasting time for TV dramas at TV stations should be strictly controlled to 42–45 minutes. Once uploaded on the Internet, however, webisodes can be watched at any time, so gradually, TV dramas are also put on online platforms.

Yang: Communication with the platform was one of the biggest challenges I faced because I had no such experience before. Once you finish a TV series and someone buys it, you can breakeven and even make profits. As for movies, the profits rely on sales of movie tickets which verify their popularity among the audience. But for online movies and webisodes, it depends on whether the platform loves this work or not. And you play a passive role in the relationship, which means you have to obey these platform's requirement. What makes it painful is that they are not professional in the process and often boss you around. They make you extremely uncomfortable.

Q7: What's the difference between the creations of TV series, webisode and film?

Bo: Duration, and it also shows lots of problems. For instance, film has the shortest duration, so the key to successful work is the idea you conveyed, or in other words, your creativity. Do you have an impressive story, or do the characters have a strong, striking force that can impress the audience? We tend to believe film is the creation of the director, since the style of the director will be greatly reflected in the final product. In addition, since the total words of a film script are much fewer than that of TV series or webisodes, 20,000 to 40,000 to be exact, the cost of rewriting is small, which leads to the little saying of a scriptwriter in film production. By contrast, the story is totally different in TV series or webisode. A drama series script usually has 450,000 words in total, which is difficult to rewrite again. Hence, our scriptwriters have much saying in this field.

Qin and Wang: Online literature contains some edgy content, which has attracted a number of readers. As a result, the platforms are only interested in the themes related to online literature. Many TV companies have bought lots of IPs, using them for webisode and game development. At first, the IPs can produce projects that are quite good. But then, the government imposed censoring rules, and about 50 percent of the IPs can't be broadcasted. Since the money had already been spent on IPs, TV companies would like to take advantage of their value, so they begin to find someone to adapt it, using the name of IP and its characters, but rewriting the plot. However, it turns out to be a failure, with few projects being successful, and producers being restricted by the content. In fact, what investors want is the original IPs, and this leads to contradictions—the original content can't be broadcasted, and the adaptation is not satisfactory. The current situation is that a large number of IPs have been wasted. While some types of IPs can be broadcasted, their plots are similar, and there are certain formulae to follow, for example, a bossy president as the male protagonist or a tense relationship between a couple as sources of conflicts.

Now, online platforms have taken the initiative. Gradually, three forms of cooperation between producers and platforms are developed: The first form is called self-produced project, which means that the projects are completely made by the online platform itself. For example, if there is a very good IP, the platform will organize production companies or online studios to carry out the projects. The IP is chosen based on the big data, and has also been recognized by the editorial board of the platform. It may find screenwriters and directors from outside, but the copyright totally belongs to the platform. There are two kinds of self-produced projects. One is a profit-sharing project: suppose a company has a very good IP, and would like to cooperate with the platform to develop a project. After evaluation, the platform says it can be used and gives the company money, then the company gets the project done. In this case, the ratio of profit is divided, but the platform has the leading role in the cooperation. Another type is the top series. The platforms usually release one top series each month.[2]

---

2 For more detailed discussion about top series, please go to Q11.

Q8: National Radio and Television Administration (NRTA) is currently promoting the production of short drama within 30 episodes, and encouraging the company to cut the drama under 40 episodes. How will this policy affect the creation and production of webisodes? What kinds of impact does it have on your work?

Bo: I think it's good. Just like the American TV series, maybe the first season is very exciting, and the second season is about the same. Few TV series and webisode are great in every season. Generally, the longer your plot, the harder can it be impressive. For a drama that is about family, it may be easier, while for others, it is not. Plus, almost everyone knows that the company is selling episodes on a mortgage, so they want the drama longer so as to earn more money. Now, what NRTA did was helpful to improve this situation. As a scriptwriter, I surely don't want any useless scene to appear in the drama as the whole story has already been clear and complete. But suddenly, you add some plots that are not meant to be here, which disrupts my pace and all the organized scenes. *Yang:* It does not affect webisodes but has an impact on the TV series. Webisodes usually do not have many episodes, and a season is composed of 12 episodes. But to reduce the costs, the TV series has many episodes. If the investment of a TV series is 5,000,000 yuan per episode, the total cost will be calculated according to 30 episodes. Actors are paid on an episode basis. For unfamous actors, they will receive the remuneration of 30 episodes. The TV series will have 40 or even more than 70 episodes. And the extra episodes are to spread the cost. Now the number of episodes is limited to less than 40, and 30 will be preferred.

Q9: Could you tell me how the production side contacts the platforms? Or do you have some advice on how to contact the platform? Do you have any skills in communicating with the platform?

Qing and Wang: First, the large-scale production companies and the platforms have equal status in the partnership. Platforms are willing to cooperate with established film and TV production companies as previous dramas produced by these companies are well received and they have the resources of social capital, directors, professional personnel, scripts and IPs. An example is *Qing Yu Nian*. As it is an excellent IP, the company invites people to make it, and the platform is the major investor. After negotiating with platforms, the proportion of profit-sharing can be decided. Second, well-known scriptwriters often communicate with platforms and share their ideas with them. For example, Yu Zheng, one of the top screenwriters, has a good relationship with Hunan TV station, so his TV dramas were often broadcasted on Hunan TV in the past. Now his works are mainly released on the online video platform. If platforms are interested in Yu Zheng's work, they will assign him to be in charge of the project, invest in it and cooperate with him to produce it. The overall profits are calculated according to the number of episodes and then shared. That is to say, if renowned producers, screenwriters and early development managers maintain a good relationship with each other, their cooperation will be reached. There is another kind of situation when the platform has a good IP and has a clear idea of who is suitable for writing this theme. Therefore, the platform will talk with the screenwriter about the cooperation in developing the script. An agreement will be signed if the screenwriter is interested in the book after reading it. But the screenwriter is required to write an outline and five episodes of the entire series first so that further negotiation is possible. Although the conditions are the same as others, the platforms will come to the screenwriter as long as they have an IP, and won't accept outlines and scripts developed by other screenwriters. There is also a kind of famous scriptwriters like Qin Shuang who have written an outline and shared their ideas with platforms. In the past, if platforms thought highly of the ideas, they would cooperate with the scriptwriter and decide the remuneration for each episode and mode of payment. But now, even if your idea is good, you need to write an outline first, and then both parties can sign a contract if the platform is satisfied with the outline. After that, it will be regarded as the platform's top series, and scriptwriters also need to deliver the scripts on time.

Q10: According to data, some online video platforms have lost 3.4 billion, with a minimum loss about 1 billion. Do the platforms do this to keep ranking in the upper reaches? It has been a vicious circle. Does the current alliance mean to help one other to get out of difficulties? The people who visit online platform are young and they usually are less well-off. Compared with the membership system of foreign media, China's membership charges less. Is this profit model feasible?

> *Qing and Wang:* First of all, this situation may be adjusted in the future. Because the standards of online platforms have become the same as TV stations, people are more willing to use mobile phones and computers to watch dramas. In this case, the business of TV stations has shrunk by 75 to 80 percent. Three top online video platforms have brought a certain blow to the 45 TV stations, and advertisers have basically gone to cooperate with the platforms. Although the platforms are still losing money in terms of advertising expenses, the cost of buying dramas and the income from membership and click rate, what investors aim at is the future of the platforms. With the data and money in place, each of the three platforms has other ways to make profits. Secondly, it is common for Chinese people to watch dramas when they go to the toilet, eat or lie down. But for foreigners, watching TV is to sit down before the television

and then enjoy the drama slowly. This is very different from Chinese habits. Therefore, foreign TV stations can develop steadily and they are also under the protection of the government, which forms a virtuous circle. In the past, there were thousands of TV stations in China, which had formed a vicious competition. In terms of films, foreign directors value good image, lighting and sound qualities, and then the audience is bound to feel the impact of the pictures, but Chinese viewers pay more attention to content. The strategy taken by the online video and e-commerce platforms is to kill TV stations and then movie theaters. About 90 percent of the tickets are sold online by e-commerce now. The investors themselves are Maoyan Entertainment, Taopiaopiao and so on, who are making money from selling movie tickets and investing in film productions, then it becomes making money from both sides for them. In fact, like Netflix, many films are released directly online, which is likely to limit the development of the film industry.

Q11: How top series and self-produced series are produced by the platforms? Any observations you can share with me?

Qing and Wang: Talking back to the top series, the online platform absolutely has the initiative. For self-produced series, there might still be possibilities for others to invest. There are several models to produce top series. If a platform wants to produce top series but without enough ability to produce on its own, then it will assign projects to a bunch of so-called studios, which maintain some close relationships with acting agencies and production companies. Another type is that a traditional TV production company, like New Classics Media, which has relatively strong productivity, and after years of development has completed the primitive accumulation with its own actors and all kinds of contacts, will also cooperate with the online platform, that is, both parties will make the production together, then broadcast the webisodes on the platform. In the case of making top series, the platforms will be the dominant investor and air the webisodes produced by the company, while in the case of self-produced series, the company will be the co-investor with the platforms. All top TV production companies in the market have already cooperated with online video platforms in this way. Another situation is that the production company negotiates with the online platform and wants to put the online drama series onto the platform, then the profit-sharing model will be taken and the profit will be divided according to click rate. In this case, there's a 98 percent chance you won't get paid, and only a 2 percent chance for the online drama series to make a profit, if it can become a dark horse. As a result, very few companies are willing to choose the profit-sharing model, and the first model becomes monopolistic.

CONTENT, PLATFORMS AND DISTRIBUTION

And now, platforms have begun to communicate with one another; for example, platform A evaluates one online drama series to be RMB 3 million per episode, then it will inform other platforms about this situation; therefore, no platforms will provide prices more than 3 million. When such communication was not formed, it was possible that one platform would provide 3 million, and another would provide 3.5 million to compete, thus there was a chance for the rising budget. However, once the information is shared, there is no such opportunity, for no platform wants to pay more. Now, after forming an alliance, the price is fixed and the vicious competition is avoided.

Another thing is that, some platforms have partner companies that can provide corresponding services, for example, if the partner company is an acting agency, the platform can invest a total of RMB 6 million for the extras, then both parties sign an agreement and the acting agency brings the platform all the invoices. The acting agency ensures the recruitment of actors, while if it is a script company, then it will be responsible for the writing of scripts. This kind of business model is very convenient for the online platform, but can easily breed corruption. For example, 1 million kickback could be for a 7 million contract. For some 500 million project, the kickback could even reach 50 million if it is 10 percent of the whole budget. The platform has the dominant power. For certain cases, even though you probably occupy 49 percent of the investment and the platform 51 percent, you have to listen to the platform because the platform is the one that purchases the final product. You are counting on the platform to make money. I think such a corruption phenomenon is very serious, and I dare not say it openly. There are only three top online platforms, and if you expose the corruption, you will never have the chance to cooperate with them again.

Yao: There are two different business models for us: customized series and profit-sharing series. The customized series has a larger scale and greater influence, while the interest is comparatively lower and the filming time longer. With its large scale, the customized series requires higher communication cost and longer filming time, for two years or more. Besides, there is no guarantee for the success of customized series, so you cannot work on dozens of customized series, for it is possible that some of them, after negotiation for a year or two, can not be carried out at the end. While the profit-sharing project has a smaller scale, for example, mainstream profit-sharing webisode take RMB 20-30 million, in which the platform plays a smaller role, so I think the business model is B2B combined with B2C. In the profit-sharing project, the filming crew has more subjectivity, and we negotiate with the platform about how and when to release the drama after we finish the project, so the communication cost is lower and the filming time shorter. Above all, it'd be better for us to work on both types of projects.

Q12: Have you carried out any profit-sharing projects? How do you avoid the risks in those projects?

Yao: I cannot say I avoided all risks, but all the profit-sharing projects did make money. Also, this will become a trend, since it is a healthier business model for the platforms and they are also promoting this model.

Q13: But other interviewees said they will not work on profit-sharing project anymore. Do you think they are too conservative?

Yao: Many said the profit-sharing projects are harder than other models. This is true in the whole market; for example, in movie industry, only 10 or 20 percent of projects profit, but there are still many people making movies. So, the only question is whether you have the confidence to produce top series.

Q14: What do you think about the current situation of production management in the film and television industry?

Yang: The access threshold of our industry in China is so low that everyone can participate in it, regardless of their age, education and professional background. For example, if you can get investment, you can be a producer or director. Frankly speaking, there is a shortage of professionalism in our industry. Many staff haven't received professional training and they even fail to understand the request of directors. I think professional certificates are required to ensure the professionalism of workers. And in South Korea and Japan, most workers are graduated from the academy and work from a grassroot level. But in China, we at least start to work as assistant cameraman and assistant director, instead of starting from the bottom to get enough work experience. When I went to South Korea to learn how they shoot films, I found they are very professional and the number of staff in each crew is less than ours. In China, there are 700 to 800 or even 1,000 people in a crew. When I shot *Forever Enthralled* in 2007, our crew only had 400 workers. As the labor of division becomes finer, today shooting a film needs large number of people. When I worked as a makeup artist for *Dream of the Red Chamber* in the 1980s, I was responsible for makeup and hair design. But now more professionals are needed, like makeup, special makeup artist, hairstylist and stylist. Therefore, to reduce the cost, I told the stylist of my next webisode to decrease the number of workers in the makeup department.

Q15: Do you think webisodes should be close to people's lives and reflect social reality? There are many meaningless TV series now. Do you want to shoot something that can reflect social reality and cause empathy?

Yang: Yes. In China, there are many people who live a hard life, especially the epidemic has led to unemployment. Thus, they would like to watch movies that can make them happy or empathize with them. For example, in 2020, there was a movie named *A Little Red Flower*, which tells a story about two families stricken with cancer and the travails that the patients themselves and their families undergo. It is a warm and realistic film that can move the audience. And the play that I am preparing for now is about the postnatal care center. As the director I hire is Korean, I am applying for his Chinese visa. If the application can be approved this month, he will come to China to make preparations for the play. The reason for making this webisode is that young people today have different ideas of confinement in childbirth from us. It is worth considering whether it is necessary to practice confinement after the birth of a child or not. In Western countries, there is no such tradition. As for young people, they prefer to have confinement in the postnatal care center. Therefore, this theme is related to our life and can strike chords with the audience. We invite the Korean director to ensure it is an affectional drama series as we expected instead of a soap opera.

Q16: What are the biggest challenges and difficulties of webisode in 2021? As a scriptwriter, do you have any predictions or ideas about the types of webisodes needed online?

Bo: The control and regulation for this field would be stricter, especially in terms of the themes. For example, in the past, you may be able to earn some money by making sexual-related webisodes, but now it is impossible. However, on the other hand, most of the content and plots are generated from the folk, and therefore wild. Then the audience's preferences are directly spawned. These things are unrefined, but full of vigor. So, too many government regulations somehow restricted the creativity of webisodes. Someone says that online literature before 2017 and 2018 is much better than that of now. It would happen to webisodes too as too much censorship would gradually lead to the disappearance of the richness of subject matters.

Another point is I think, a webisode is hard to predict. Like before *The Bad Kids* came out, I could never imagine seeing this kind of drama. And this happens every year. The second point is the theme of female power is getting into the public. This is especially obvious in Korean drama. Many Korean dramas now are talking about equal rights in various fields, for example, sexual harassment in the office and life. Generally, it is the trend. Females are thinking about questions like what kinds of life I want to live, etc. Another trend I think would be those positive drama that are warm and healing. One is, amid the economic downturn, people don't like to see dramas about fights or things like that; the other is that because of the pandemic, it's impossible for people to gather together and start some big plays. So I think there must be some dramas that use the best actors, photographers, music directors to reflect the image of our great country. More and more, for sure.

Q17: Do you cooperate with the platform directly? Or do other staff like the producer have to get involved? Sometimes, a scriptwriter has to make lots of compromises even if he or she knows what the platform advocates is wrong. I know some small screenwriters who end up with depression since they think no one appreciates their work, and the only thing they are asked to do is to revise again and again. What do you think of this phenomenon?

Bo: No matter what kinds of drama you make, eventually, we will have to cooperate with the platform. Now, producers don't have much authority. Basically, now they just focus on producing the video, which I think is not good.

Originally the producer had lots of functions: control the overall process of production; decide the style of the product; look for partners; let every department cooperate perfectly; most importantly, they understand drama and casts. They are working as a mediator to solve the problems between supply and demand. However, the website and platform are so powerful that they finish most of the things that were originally done by producers. Therefore, our scriptwriters have to face the first party by ourselves, and they communicate with us directly too. But the tricky thing is, these platforms don't understand how drama works, how the scripts work, so it's hard for us to explain to them, and it's difficult to tell them, "your idea is absurd." It just doesn't work like that.

Same thing happens to the director. They used to have lots of saying on a project, including mediating between the creator and the customers, producing new ideas, etc. But now it is the platform telling you what should be done, what the work should be like. This puts lots of pressure on the scriptwriter, since we are just a second party, and it's hard for us to contend with the platform. Thus it's basically impossible for us to insist on our ideas and concepts.

I understand the phenomenon you mentioned. Luckily I have a strong heart, and usually, I'm sure I'm right. This has nothing to do with your professional literacy. To be honest, I'm upset when some casts and platforms give many suggestions. How much time did you spend thinking about this script? It's impossible for a cast or a platform to consider a script like mine for four to five years. I'm not an idiot; even if our ideas may not be better than yours, they must be more comprehensive. So I won't believe I'm wrong, and it's clear to me where they are wrong. It's just a matter of persistence. There will be many obstacles, but in the end, you'll find nobody cares about this work more than you do since your name will be on the work. The netizens don't know who told you to revise the script. The fact is, they will only scorn and curse you with disgusting words when they are dissatisfied with the drama. What you can do is insist on our ideas until the last moment.

Fortunately, I make a lot of money, at least in the field of writing. I still remember an actor telling me that he counts the time waiting at the scene into his salary, since during shooting, the production assistant often woke him up at 4 a.m., preparing all the staff like makeup, changing costumes, while ended up waiting a whole morning not acting in even one scene. He earns the "waiting money" instead of "acting money." The same principle applies to scriptwriters as well. I enjoy writing scripts, so I don't make money from that; instead, I earn from revising my script. Revising is a torture.

Conclusion

From the above points of view, there is no doubt that the development history of Chinese online drama is tortuous and complicated. There are various opinions on the origin of Chinese network drama production, and there are not many authoritative, relevant research documents.

At present, there are several opinions about the origin of Chinese web series: Chinese web series originated from simple UGC video works, the most famous of which is the 2005 short film *A Bloody Case Caused by a Steamed Bun* which criticized Chen Kaige's film *The Promise*; Chinese web series originated from relatively complex PGC video works, the most famous of which is the 2007 Shanghai TV web series *Crazy*; Chinese web series originated from simple UGC original video works, the most famous of which is *Primary Colors*, which was written, directed and performed by five college students at the cost of 2,000 yuan in the year 2000 (Wang, 2019).

Which of these three statements is more convincing? This begs the question: Do web dramas belong to UGC or PGC? From the perspective of the interviewees in this study, web series belong to PGC works. Therefore, this study can believe that the development of online drama originated from the 2007 Shanghai TV network drama *Crazy*. But there is no doubt that these three online dramas belong to the works with low production costs and marginal topics proposed by Bo.

The following year, the State Administration of Radio, Film and Television and the Ministry of Information Industry (both of which have since been restructured) issued the Regulation on the Administration of Internet Audiovisual Program Services, which is believed to be China's first legal document regulating webisode (Dong, 2016). The legal document stipulates that online audiovisual programs should not contain 10 items of prohibited content, including "inducing minors to break the law and commit crimes, and promoting violence, pornography, gambling and terrorist activities."

However, it is possible to overestimate the legal document's historical significance. As early as 2004, the State Administration of Radio, Film and Television promulgated the Administrative Measures for Audiovisual Programs Transmitted through the Internet and other Information Networks, which can also be understood as China's first regulation of the order of audiovisual programs transmitted through the Internet and other information networks, including online dramas. The regulation stipulates that audiovisual programs of movies and TV dramas that are to be distributed to the public through Internet must obtain a TV drama distribution license or a film release license.

In a word, there is no doubt that the Regulations on the Administration of Internet Audiovisual Program Services and the Measures on the Administration of Internet and Other Information Network Communication Audiovisual Programs have milestone significance in the history of Chinese webisode regulation, but the exact status of these two regulations in the history of Chinese network drama regulation is still unclear. Although these laws and regulations have to some extent eliminated the liberalism of online dramas, they have also established the legitimacy of the online drama industry and promoted the birth and development of original webisode independently produced by video websites (hereinafter referred to as self-made webisode/online drama).

Self-made original webisode refers to those webisode that are independently selected by video websites for subject matter, script conception, shooting and post-production, and broadcast mainly through online platforms (Song, 2017). In 2009, Tudou launched the black detective webisode *Mr. Lei*, which is similar to the traditional TV series in terms of production techniques and series form, and is considered as the first domestic online self-made drama in the industry. Furthermore, with the popularization of the Internet and the development of the film and television industry, the conceptual boundaries between webisode and TV series are becoming blurred in terms of production techniques, drama forms and even communication channels.

In addition, in this study, the concept of online drama and self-made online drama is often confused, but when the interviewees talk about the status quo and the future of online drama, the concept of self-made online drama is basically equivalent to online drama. This also undoubtedly reveals the development of the industry dynamics.

To sum up, the development of online drama cannot be separated from the changes in the supervision of online drama. Meanwhile, the acceleration of media integration is making online drama become mainstream from non-mainstream. From the perspective of the regulatory history of online series, it is not difficult to find that the changes Qin and Wang reported in 2015 and 2018 are no longer within the time frame when the above laws were promulgated. But in 2015, as Qin and Wang reported, China's online drama regulation also faced a major turning point. At a major industry conference in 2015, the State Administration of Radio, Film and Television declared that "the Internet cannot broadcast content that is not allowed on television." This remark is an important signal to strengthen the management of online drama and network homemade programs.

The following year, eight popular online dramas, including *Go Princess Go*, *Psychological Crime* and *Soul Ferry*, were removed by regulators. However, the respondents in this study did not make clear the authorities' increasingly strict supervision of online drama, which may be due to the following reasons: at that time, the regulatory standards of online drama were not clear, the construction of the regulatory system of online drama was still at the downstream of the industrial chain and the functions of the regulatory enforcement department of online drama were not yet clear (Xu & Wang, 2017). Obviously, at that time, the immature but increasingly strict regulation of online drama actually raised the profit risk of the industry, and the authorities' usual concept of censorship of old media, namely television, was not in line with the user-centered business concept of audiovisual content of new media, so the growth style of online drama became increasingly conservative (Xu & Wang, 2017). Therefore, Qin and Wang stressed that the era of user-centered business concepts providing creative ideas for online TV series to win at a low cost is gone.

Qin and Wang also believe that after 2018, famous actors who are good at acting are more actively participating in the high-quality development of online dramas. This is closely related to an official talk that year. The National TV Drama Creation Planning Conference was held by Nie Chenxi, director of the NRTA, and this meeting is also the first national TV drama creation planning conference held by the NRTA after the name change and restructuring, which shows the importance of this meeting. And the TV series mentioned in this meeting actually refers to series including web series. The conference emphasized one thing in particular, that is: eliminate the redundant production phenomenon of TV series industry and further improve the quality of TV series. Scholars' comments on the development of online dramas in recent years are also consistent with the comments of the interviewees in this study. Scholars believe that the output of Chinese online dramas has increased steadily in recent years, the subject types of Chinese online dramas have become diversified, the content quality of Chinese online dramas has been improved comprehensively and phenomenon online dramas have also appeared frequently (Gao, 2019; Hao, 2015).

References

Cheng, Ruyan 程汝雁. 2019. 'Qianxi Duanshiping Fengkouxia Wangluo Zizhiju de Tiaozhan yu Chuangxin 浅析短视频风口下网络自制剧的挑战与创新' ['Brief Analysis of the Challenge and Innovation of Network Homemade Drama Under the Draught of Short Video']. *Journal of News Research* 16: 104–105.

Chin Chan, Yik. 2011. 'Policy Process, Policy Learning, and the Role of the Provincial Media in China.' *Media, Culture & Society* 33 (2): 193–210.

Dong, Youheng 董有恒. 2016. 'Wangju Jingbo Shijian de Faxue Sikao 网剧禁播事件的法学思考' ['Legal Thoughts on the "Forbidden Broadcast" Event of Network Dram']. *Modern Business Trade Industry* 22: 128–129. doi:10.19311/j.cnki.1672-3198.2016.22.062.

Feng, Guangchao Charles and Steve Zhongshi Guo. 2013. 'Tracing the Route of China's Internet Censorship: An Empirical Study.' *Telematics and Informatics* 30 (4): 335–345.

Freeman, M. 2016. *Industrial Approaches to Media: A Methodological Gateway to Industry Studies*. London: Palgrave MacMillan.

Gao, Yuting 高玉婷. 2019. 'Fufei Moshi xia Wangju Neirong Shengchan de Tisheng Lujin 付费模式下网剧内容生产的提升路径' ['The Promotion Path of Online Drama Content Production Under the Pay Model']. *A Vast View on Publishing* 6: 73–75. doi:10.16491/j.cnki.cn45-1216/g2.2019.06.022.

Hao, Ye 郝烨. 2015. 'Zhongguo Wangluo Zizhiju Fazhan Xianzhuang yu Duice 中国网络自制剧发展现状与对策' ['Development Status and Countermeasures of Chinese Network Self-made Drama']. *Contemporary Film* 11: 150–152.

Hu, Tingting, and Cathy Y. Wang. 2020. 'Who is the Counterpublic? Bromance-as-Masquerade in Chinese Online Drama—S.C.I. Mystery.' *Television & New Media* 22 (6): 671–686. doi:10.1177/1527476420937262.

Leng, Song and Zhang, Liping 张丽平, 冷淞. 2015. 'Zhongguo Wangluo Zizhiju de Fazhan yu Weilai Zouxiang 中国网络自制剧的发展与未来走向' ['The Development and Future Trend of Chinese Network Homemade Dramas']. *Beijing: Contemporary TV* 4: 11–12.

Li, Danlin 李丹林. 2012. 'Meijie Ronghe Shidai Chuanmei Guanzhi Wenti de Sikao – Jiyu Gonggong Liyi Yuanze de Fenxi 媒介融合时代传媒管制问题的思考——基于"公共利益"原则的分析' ['Reflections on media Regulation in the Era of Media Convergence -- An Analysis based on the Principle of Public Interest']. *Modern Communication* 34 (5): 10–14.

Li, Danyang 李丹. 2020. 'Neirong Zhizuo Yingxiao Wangluoju Shengchanlian Xianzhuang Jiedu Duihua Dianshiju Yingyan Neirong ZhuguanZouchunran 内容·制作·营销：网络剧生产链现状解读——对话 "电视剧鹰眼" 内容主管邹春然' ['Content · Production · Marketing: An interpretation of the current situation of network drama production chain -- A dialogue with Zou Chunran, content director of "TV Drama Eagle Eye"']. *Modern Audio-Video Arts* 3: 27–29.

Lv, Meng Min 吕梦明. 2019. 'Cong Maikuier de Shouzhong Lilun Shijiao Fenxi Dianshiju he Wangju de Chayi 从麦奎尔的受众理论视角分析电视剧和网剧的差异' ['From the Perspective of McGuire's Audience Theory Analyzes the Differences Between TV Series and Network Dramas']. *Radio & TV Journal* 7: 12–13.

Potter, Anna. 2018. 'Managing Productive Academia/Industry Relations: The Interview as Research Method.' *Media Practice and Education* 19 (2): 159–172.

Shen, Wei. 2012. 'Deconstructing the Myth of Alipay Drama—Repoliticizing Foreign Investment in the Telecommunications Sector in China.' *Telecommunications Policy* 36 (10–11): 929–942.

Song, Bing Hua 宋秉华. 2020. 'Lun Zhongguo Wangluo Zizhiju Yingxiao de Yingli Moshi 论中国网络自制剧营销的盈利模式' ['On the Profit Model of Chinese Network Homemade Drama Marketing']. *Modern Audio-Video Arts* (11): 44–48.

Song, Peiying 宋培英. 2017. '国内网络自制剧的历史现状与突围路径 Guonei Wangluo Zizhiju de Lishi Xianzhuang yu Tuwei Lujin' ['The History, Present Situation and Breakthrough Path of Domestic Network Self-made Drama']. *Journal of Chinese Radio and Television* 4: 85–88.

Tang, Rui Feng 唐瑞峰. 2019. 'Guangdian Zongju Kaizhan Guangbo Dianshi Jiemu he Dianshiju Zhizuo Huanzheng Gongzuo Wangluo Shiting Jiemu Xinxi Beian Xitong Shengji 广电总局开展广播电视节目和电视剧制作换证工作网络视听节目信息备案系统升级' ['The State Administration of Radio, Film and Television Upgraded the Online Audio-Visual Program Information Filing System for the Production and Replacement of Radio and TV Programs and TV Dramas']. *TV Guide* 168(04): 8–11.

Tian, Weigang and Zhang, Rudong 田维钢,张如东. 2017. 'Hulianwang Shiting Jiemu Neirong Jianguan Fenxi – Yi Meijie Guifan Lilun wei Shijiao 互联网视听节目内容监管分析———以媒介规范理论为视角' ['Content Regulation analysis of Internet Audio-Visual Programs -- From the Perspective of Media Regulation Theory']. *Youth Journalist* 22: 78–79.

Wang, Han 王涵. 2020. '2020 Nian Wangluoju Diaoyan Baogao Wangtai Fenjiexian Zhenzheng Fenjie 年网络剧调研报告 网台分界线真正"分解",网剧地位迈上新台阶' ['2020 Network Drama Research Report Network Station Demarcation Line Really "decomposition", Network Drama Status to a New Level']. *TV Guide* 21: 32–39.

Wang, Tianyu 王天瑜. 2017. 'Wangshang Wangxia Tongyi Biaozhun de Guanli Shijian 网上网下统一标准的管理实践———对《关于进一步加强网络视听节目创作播出管理的通知》的理解' ['Management Practice of Unified Standards on and off the Internet -- Understanding of "Notice on Further Strengthening Management of Creation and Broadcast of Network Audio-Visual Programs"']. *Sheng Ping Shijie* 8: 17–20.

Wang, Wenjing 王文静. 2019. 'Wangluoju Chuangzuo Chuanbo Zhong dui Xianshi de Xuhua yu Jujiao 网络剧创作传播对现实的虚化与聚焦' ['The Blurring and Focusing of Reality in the Creation and Communication of Network Drama']. *Chinese Literature and Art Review* 3: 75–85.

Wen, Hu, Zhang, Qiangguo. and Su, Xu 文嫮, 张强国, 粟旭. 2020. 'Hulianwang Yingxiang Xiade Wangju yu Chuantong Taiju Shengchan Wangluo de Jiegou Cha yi 互联网影响下的"网剧"与传统"台剧"生产网络的结构差异' ['The Structural Differences Between "Net Drama" and Traditional "Taiwan Drama" Production Networks Under the Influence of the Internet']. *Geographical Research* 6: 1329–1342.

Xi, Jingping 习近平. 2016. 'Zai Wangluo Anquan he Xinxihua Gongzuo Zuotanhui shang de Jianghua (习近平)在网络安全和信息化工作座谈会上的讲话' ['Xi's Speech at the Symposium on Network Security and Informatization Work']. *China Emergency Management* 4: 12–16.

Xiao, Yingying and Xu, Xinyu 萧盈盈 许心雨. 2017. 'Yangcheng Youzhi Neirong Dazao Wangluoju Shengtai Bihuan – Zhuanfang Aiqiyi Fuzongcai Wangluoju Zizhi Kaifa Zhongxin Zongjingli Daiyin 养成优质内容,打造网络剧生态闭环—

—专访爱奇艺副总裁、网络剧自制开发中心总经理戴莹' ['Develop High-Quality Content, Build an Ecological Closed-Loop Network Drama -- Interview with Dai Ying, Vice President of IQiyi, General Manager of Network Drama Development Center']. *South China Television Journal* 5: 18–21.

Xu, Yaping and Wang, Xue 徐亚萍, 王雪. 2017. 'Wangluo Zizhiju de Fazhan Jiqi Xingzheng Guizhi Guanli Fengxian 网络自制剧的发展及其行政规制管理风险' ['The Development of Network Homemade Drama and Its Administrative Regulation Management Risk']. *Modern Audio-Video Arts* 3: 29–37.

Zhan, Di and Deng, Huiming 战迪, 邓慧敏. 2021. 'Hou Dianshiwang Shidai de Zhongguo Wangju Tuwei – Cong Chanyelian Dao Jiazhilian Zhuanhuan 后电视网时代"的中国网剧突围——从产业链到价值链转换' ['Breakout of Chinese Network Drama in Post-TV Era -- Transformation from Industrial Chain to Value Chain']. *Editorial Friend* 10: 74–79.

Zhang, Xuejiao 张雪娇. 2017. 'Guanyu Dianshiju Wangluoju Zhizuo Chengben Peizhi Bili de Yijian《关于电视剧网络剧制作成本配置比例的意见》发布' ['"Opinions on Allocation Ratio of Production Cost of TV Network Drama" Was Released']. *Xinjiang Xinwen Chuban Guangdian* 5: 2.

Zhao, Xing 赵兴. 2017. 'Zouchu Wangju Chuangzuo de Wanggan Wuqu 走出网剧创作的网感误区' ['Out of the Net Drama Creation of the Sense of the Misunderstanding']. *Beijing: Journal of Beijing Film Academy* 4: 49–53.

Glossary of Chinese Terms

Roman Type (pinyin)	*Chinese Characters*	*English Equivalent Terms*
Bai Ri Zhui Xiong	《白日追凶》	Day and Night
Bangni Bo	柏邦妮	Bangni BO
Bei Jing Nü Zi Tu Jian	《北京女子图鉴》	Women in Beijing
Bie Le, Wen Ge Hua	《别了, 温哥华》	Farewell, Vancouver
Bingbing Fan	范冰冰	Bingbing FAN
Bona Yingshi Jituan	博纳影视集团	Bona Film Group
Dandan Yang	杨丹丹	Dandan YANG
Ding Zhi Ju	定制剧	Customized Series
Fen Zhang Ju	分账剧	Profit-Sharing Series
Feng Xiaogang	冯小刚	Xiaogang FENG
Hairun Yingshi	海润影视	Hairun Media
Hong Lou Meng	《红楼梦》	Dream of the Red Chamber
Hua Mu Lan	《花木兰》	Mulan
Jiang Wen	姜文	Wen JIANG
Jun Yao	药军	Jun YAO
Lang Zi Yan Qing	《浪子燕青》	Prodigal Son Yan Qing
Lao Nan Hai	《老男孩》	Old Boy
Linghun Baidu	《灵魂摆渡》	Soul Ferry
Ling Yi Zhang Lian	《另一张脸》	Another Face
Liu Jin Sui Yue	《流金岁月》	My Best Friend's Story
Mei Lan Fang	《梅兰芳》	Forever Enthralled
Mikuang	《迷狂》	Crazy
Mr Lei	《Mr.雷》	Mr. Lei

(Continued)

Glossary of Chinese Terms (*Continued*)

Roman Type (pinyin)	*Chinese Characters*	*English Equivalent Terms*
Qin Shuang	秦爽	Shuang QIN
Qing Yu Nian	《庆余年》	Qing Yu Nian
Sa Jiao Nü Ren Zui Hao Ming	《撒娇女人最好命》	Women who Flirt
San Shi Er Yi	《三十而已》	Nothing But Thirty
Song Ni Yi Duo	《送你一朵小红花》	A Little Red Flower
Xiao Hong Hua		
Tai Zi Fei Sheng Zhi Ji	《太子妃升职记》	Go Princess Go
Tian Chong Ju	甜宠剧	Sweet & Romantic Drama
Tou Bu Ju	头部剧	Top Series
Wan Wan Mei Xiang Dao	《万万没想到》	Never Expected
Wang Xiaozhu	王小柱	Xiaozhu WANG
Wu Ji	《无极》	The Promise
Xia Tian De Wei Dao	《夏天的味道》	Smell of Summer
Xinli Chuanmei	新丽传媒	New Classics Media
Xinli Zui	《心理罪》	Psychological Crime
Yige Mantou Yinfa De Xuean	《一个馒头引发的血案》	A Bloody Case Caused by a Steamed Bun
Ye Jing	叶京	Jing YE
Yin Mi De Jiao Luo	《隐秘的角落》	The Bad Kids
Yong Bu Ming Mu	《永不瞑目》	Never Close My Eyes
Youku	优酷	Youku
Yuanse	《原色》	Primary Colors
Zhao Baogang	赵宝刚	Baogang ZHAO
Zi Zhi Ju	自制剧	Self-produced Drama

NOTES ON CONTRIBUTORS

Chapter 1

Zhixia Mo is a researcher at Nanfang Think Tank for Cultural Industry and a columnist on media and cultural industries in Nanfang Plus (a Chinese news media platform). Her research interests are creative industries, film culture in the Guangdong-Hong Kong-Macao Greater Bay Area and overseas communication of Chinese films.

Hui Liu is a professor of School of Media and Communication at Shenzhen University, visiting scholar in the Producer Program of School of Theatre Film and Television in University of California, Los Angeles (2015). His main research areas include entertainment and media studies, creative media industries, art and technology, films and TV productions in Hong Kong and Taiwan. He has published more than 50 articles in Literature & Art Studies, Contemporary Cinema and Film Art (in Chinese).

Chapter 2

Jia Xian is an associate professor and master's supervisor in the Department of Drama, Film and Television Literature of Meishi Film Academy of Chongqing University and a researcher of Chongqing Key Laboratory of Digital Film and Television Art Theory and Technology.

Qinqin Ren is a master degree graduate of Meishi Film Academy of Chongqing University of 2019.

Chapter 3

Xiaying Xu received his Ph.D. in communication from the University of Macau. He currently serves as an associate professor in the Public Relations and Advertising Program and associate head of the Department of Communication at BNU-HKBU United International College (UIC). His research interests include creative industries, cultural and media studies.

Qingyuan Zhao received his master degree in communication from Hong Kong Baptist University. His current research focuses on cultural and media studies, specializing in medical dramas.

Chapter 4

Wei Jiang is an associate professor teaching at BNU-HKBU United International College (UIC). He received his Ph.D. in communication from the University of Macau. His research areas focus on the Japanese representations in Chinese war films made during and after Mao's era, the Revolutionary Model Opera films in the Cultural Revolution, Chinese shadow plays and Chinese new media development. He has visited the University of Southern California on the T. C. Wang Fellowship. He has had professional experience in the Chinese film industry, having variously worked as assistant director and art department coordinator to renowned film directors such as John Woo and Jiang Wen.

Pengcheng Zhou is an Mphil student jointly supervised by Hong Kong Baptist University and UIC, and an ICA member; he presided over the completion of a research project sponsored by the National College students' Innovation and Entrepreneurship Training Program. He participated in several academic conferences held by ICA, University of Science and Technology of China, Huazhong University of Science and Technology, Beijing Film Academy, Shaanxi Normal University.

INDEX

artificial intelligence (AI) 7, 11–13, 15
audience vi–vii, 2, 5–14, 23–26, 29, 32–33, 38–41, 44–45, 52, 54, 57, 59–61, 63, 65–66, 70, 73; Chinese vi, 39; global 2; local 23, 34
audience base 10, 30, 40
audience comments 37
audience demand 8
audience differentiation 59
audience habit 22
audience loyalty 2, 11
audience market 2, 21, 31
audience positioning 14
audience preferences 60, 73
audience strategy 2, 9
audience studies ix

The Bad Kids (2020) 24, 26, 32–33, 40, 73
big data x, 12, 15, 63–64, 67
Bilibili 23, 38–39, 47
bullet screen vi, ix, 37–46, 48–52, 54
Burning Ice (2017) 40

censorship 1, 34, 58, 73, 77
Chinese model 2
Chinese online culture 38
Chinese streaming media 3
Chinese television vi–vii, x, 29
content production viii, 13, 21, 25, 30–33, 40, 57
convergence vii; culture ix, 39; media vii; technology vii
co-production vii–viii
copyright 1, 3–5, 7, 11–13, 33, 59, 67
Crime Crackdown (2021) 37, 40–43, 45–47, 51–52
Crimson River (2020) 26
critical decodings 39
Curtin, Michael vi

Danmaku 37
Day and Night (2017) 40
dual contract 62

evaluation system 64

Fan Bingbing 61
fandom 41–44
Fung, Anthony 40

genre x, 7–9, 21, 23–26, 29, 40, 46; blending 25; classification 24; drams 30–31; fusion 24–25; integration 24

Higashino, Keigo 30
homemade short dramas 29, 33

In the Name of People (2017) 40
intellectual property (IP) 1, 7–8, 59, 62, 67–69
intertextual allusions 38
intertextual comments 41, 43, 46, 54
intertextual references 44–45
intertextuality 38, 54
iQIYI vi–ix, 1–15, 19–21, 23–24, 30–33, 37, 39, 48
iQIYI's globalization strategies 1, 2, 13–15

Jenkins, Henry 39, 54

kickback 71
Kidnapping Game (2020) 24, 26–27, 29–31

The Long Night (2020) 26

Maoyan Entertainment 70
membership 2, 5–7, 9–11, 33, 45, 69
Mist Theater viii–ix, 19–34, 40
mutual aids 39

narrative innovation 24, 29
National Radio and Television Administration (NRTA) 21–23, 61, 68, 77
Netflix vi–ix, 1–3, 7–9, 14, 20, 24–25, 34, 37, 40, 45, 70

online distribution 1–2
online dramas 21–23, 57–58, 75–78
online self-made content 23, 34
operation mode 30–31, 34
original production vii–ix, 2, 7
originals 1, 2, 5, 9, 12–14
overlaid audience comments 37

pandemic 11, 34, 65, 73
platform 5, 7–11, 14–15, 19–24, 32–33, 40, 45, 48–49, 53–54, 57, 59, 62–72, 74, 76; online 3, 62, 65–67, 69–71, 76; technology oriented 5
professional-generated content (PGC) 20, 75
profit-sharing project 67, 71–72
python ix, 41, 54

quality dramas 23
Quality TV 22, 29

representation 29, 40

script 21, 30, 59–60, 62, 64, 66–67, 69, 71, 74–76
scriptwriter 60, 67–69, 73–74
self-produced project 67
Sisyphus (2020) 24, 26–27, 33

social presence 38
soft nationalism 40
spoiler comments 39, 49, 50, 54
state-platform collaboration 40
streaming media 3, 7, 9, 34
subscription-video-on-demand (SVOD) vi
suspense dramas 20, 24, 26, 30–31, 34, 40, 63

Taopiaopiao 70
tax 61
television distribution 2
Tencent Video vi, vii, 1, 3–5, 21, 23, 37–38, 41, 45, 48
textual reference 38, 41, 44–46, 54
theme 24, 27–29, 33, 53, 57, 59, 61
The Thunder (2018) 40
top series 67, 69–70, 72
TV drama vi–vii, x, 21, 23, 25, 29, 47, 58–60, 66, 68, 76–77
TV stations vii, 37, 65–66, 68

user generated content (UGC) 19–20, 75

video-streaming platforms (VSPs) vi–ix, 1–4, 7, 9, 11–13, 15–16, 37–39, 41, 48, 54
virtual living room 38

webisode vi–viii, 1, 2, 5–9, 12, 13, 15, 57–68, 70–73, 75–76; the creation and production of 68; regulations of 76; self-made 76

Youku vi–viii, 1, 3–5, 21, 23, 27, 37, 48

CPSIA information can be obtained
at www.ICGtesting.com
Printed in the USA
JSHW021329030423
R12475900001B/R124759PG39650JSX00001B/1